SABINA GIBSON

Felt Softie Parade

Sew 15 Delightful Animals

Whales, Tigers, Triceratops & More

stashBOOKS®

an imprint of C&T Publishing

Text and instructional photography copyright © 2025 by Sabina Gibson

Styled photography and artwork copyright © 2025 by C&T Publishing, Inc.

Publisher: Amy Barrett-Daffin

Creative Director: Gailen Runge

Senior Editor: Roxane Cerda

Editor: Madison Moore

Technical Editor: Helen Frost

Cover/Book Designer: April Mostek

Production Coordinator: Zinnia Heinzmann

Illustrator: Kirstie Pettersen

Photography Coordinator: Rachel Ackley

Front cover photography by Ryan Darwin and Sabina Gibson

Lifestyle photography by Ryan Darwin and Sabina Gibson;
instructional and subject photography by Sabina Gibson, unless otherwise noted

Published by Stash Books, an imprint of C&T Publishing, Inc., P.O. Box 1456, Lafayette, CA 94549

Library of Congress Cataloging-in-Publication Data

Names: Gibson, Sabina, author.

Title: Felt softie parade : sew 15 delightful animals : whales, tigers, triceratops & more / Sabina Gibson.

Description: Lafayette, CA : Stash Books, an imprint of C&T Publishing, [2025] | Summary: "Inside this book lovely sewn softies, magical, prehistoric, and everyday animals come together in a parade of creatures. Create a collection of softies in a dreamy, storybook style. Sew them from felt, make them plush, and learn to detail them with delicate embroidery and sweet expressions to transform them into meaningful works of art"-- Provided by publisher.

Identifiers: LCCN 2024045999 | ISBN 9781644035641 (trade paperback) | ISBN 9781644035658 (ebook)

Subjects: LCSH: Soft toy making--Patterns. | Soft toys. | Stuffed animals (Toys)

Classification: LCC TT174.3 .G534 2025 | DDC 745.592/4--dc23/eng/20241118

LC record available at https://lccn.loc.gov/2024045999

Printed in China

10 9 8 7 6 5 4 3 2 1

Contents

PROJECTS

Simple Elephant 26

Dream Whale 30

Rainbow Tiger 38

White Bison 46

Cloud Bear 56

Baby Brontosaurus 62

Carnival Giraffe 68

Baby Triceratops 78

Introduction

I've always loved animals. As a kid, all of my favorite stories had an animal sidekick. My bedroom was filled with stuffed plushies. As I grew older, I replaced my teddies with Lisa Frank notebooks and would spend hours drawing all my favorite beasts: whales, bears, lions, and dinosaurs. But, my drawing skills could never match the visions in my head, and so I put down my pens for a while.

It wasn't until much later in life that I had the idea to sew myself a bear. Not a traditional teddy, but a woodland bear that stood on four legs. I quickly drafted a pattern and cut apart an old wool coat, and a few hours later my very first bear was standing proudly on my desk. It felt like the first time all the ideas in my mind could be created in real life. This new passion opened a whole new world for me as an animal artist.

From my earliest days selling on Etsy to illustrating picture books with my softies, I have spent thirteen years making soft animals. I've packed all that knowledge into these pages. I am so very thrilled to share my passion for this craft with you. I hope that you will find a project that sparks your imagination and brings you as much joy as these creatures have brought me.

How to Use This Book

This book contains fifteen animal projects with full step-by-step instructions, how-to photos, and patterns. But, before you dig into creating them, learn and review the basic knowledge you'll need for all of the projects in Basic Techniques (page 10) as well as the supplies you need in Tools and Materials (page 7).

The projects are also customizable—with paint and embroidery, you'll be able to make unique expressions and embellishments for your animals. Choose or mix and match any of the designs in the Embroidery Motif Library (page 22) when you make your projects.

Tools and Materials

Cut, Sew, and Stuff

The softies are created in three simple stages: cutting out the pattern pieces, sewing them together, and stuffing the animals. If you're new to sewing, there are only a few absolutely required tools. I suggest you begin with what you have accessible to you, building up your toolkit as you take on additional projects.

Wool Felt

All of the animals are made from wool felt. This is the most important material, so I suggest you invest in high-quality felt that will make your softies look and feel good. Merino wool felt is my preferred choice for its lush softness, durability, and rich colors. The fabric is flexible and forgiving, but also sturdy and strong. It's easy to find online from independent wool felt suppliers in endless colors and amounts.

Faux Fur

Some of the animals additionally use longer pile faux fur for tails and manes. For longer fur, I use long pile mongolian faux fur, and for shorter fur, I use 6mm viscose fur. These are not the only two options that will work, but both of these furs are available in a range of colors online.

Fabric Pencil or Marker

A marking tool that can be removed with heat, water, or an eraser is important for tracing the pattern pieces onto the wool felt. They are also helpful for drawing expressions onto the animals before actually stitching. I like fabric pens best, but on darker colored felts you will want a fabric pencil. If you don't have these things on hand, I find a light colored pencil works just as well!

Scissors

A good pair of fabric scissors will save you a lot of frustration. I suggest a pair on the smaller side since you'll be cutting out small pieces for the animals. An additional small pair of snips or scissors to use next to your sewing machine is very helpful.

Hand-Sewing Needle and Thread

Even if you're sewing the animals on your sewing machine, you'll still need hand-sewing tools for closing gaps and stitching expressions. You can also use the hand-sewing needle to embroider on the animals. I use common polyester thread to sew the softie, and embroidery floss for the embroidery. I prefer an embroidery needle for all hand sewing.

Sewing Pins

Like with any sewing project, it's helpful to have sewing pins to secure things in place as you work.

Sewing Machine and Thread

I use a sewing machine to sew all of the projects in the book, but if you prefer, you can also sew them by hand. Your sewing machine only needs basic straight stitch capability, and I suggest using all-purpose thread that matches or complements the felt of your project.

Polyfill or Wool Stuffing

Polyfill or natural wool stuffing are both great options for the animals. The stuffing needs to be easy to manipulate since it has to be distributed evenly and densely through the small animal body.

Details and Finishing

DMC Embroidery Floss

Many of the animals are embellished with embroidered motifs from the Embroidery Motif Library (page 22). I stitch all of these designs with DMC embroidery floss, which comes in a wide variety of colors, is high quality, and can be separated into fewer strands for finer stitching lines.

Super Glue

I use super glue to attach the spines together on the Baby Stegosaurus (page 110). This is a good way to attach tiny pieces together when you don't want any visible stitches. A little goes a long way! I use Loctite or Gorilla Glue brands.

Acrylic Gouache Paint and Brushes

Painting white felt creates beautiful and unique coloring for the animals, and has inspired many of my favorite designs, like the Cloud Bear (page 56) and Carnival Giraffe (page 68). Acrylic gouache is my preferred paint type, as it's nicely water soluble, but still provides permanent color. I use the brand Holbein, and suggest starting with just 2–3 bright colors once you decide to create a painted project. Any round, medium-sized paintbrushes will work.

Additional Supplies

When working with paint, you'll also need a small spray bottle for misting color, rubbing alcohol, and a hand towel that you don't mind getting messy. You may also find a chopstick or other similar tool helpful for turning the animals right side out.

Basic Techniques

This section contains everything you need to know to start making stuffies! The tips and techniques listed here can be applied to all the projects in this book.

Let's start with the ABC's of animal making!

Tracing and Cutting

Using Templates

The first step of creating any softie is to prepare the pattern pieces. First, access the templates you need by using the pieces in Templates (page 122). In that chapter, you can also access the templates as a downloadable PDF.

Cut out the individual paper pattern pieces for the animal you want to create. Each template includes pattern marks. Make sure to transfer them over to your fabric pattern pieces when you cut them out (see right). The pattern marks should be used to align the pieces as you sew. They are also referenced in the project instructions as indications of when to start and stop sewing.

The templates also have a sewing line. This line is ¼″ from the edge of the pattern pieces. If you want to follow the sewing line instead of worrying about seam allowance as you sew the irregular shapes, transfer it to your pattern pieces. Or, omit it and use a ¼″ seam allowance as your guide while you sew.

Finally, there are also templates for the embroidery motifs that maintain a hand-drawn look. You can use these to transfer the simple embroidery designs onto the felt with a marking tool. Or, use them as a size reference and freehand the designs for your own touch!

Fabric Pattern Pieces

Lay the paper pattern pieces on top of a sheet of wool felt. If the animal requires multiple colors of felt, make sure to check the project instructions to know which pieces should go on which colors. Arrange the pieces to maximize the use of the felt, eliminating waste fabric. I always try to cut pieces (especially small ones) from my scraps before using a new piece of felt! Whenever you are cutting two of the same template, mirror the template (turn it over to the wrong side) for the second piece.

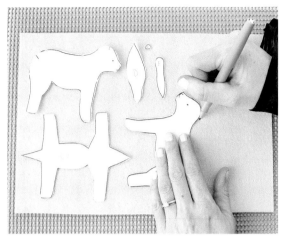

Secure the paper pieces to the felt with pins, pattern weights (small metal washers work great for this), or your hand. Then, using your fabric marking tool, trace the outline of each pattern piece onto the felt. Make sure to transfer over all pattern marks. Finally, cut out the pieces.

Sewing

Once you have the pieces ready, it's time to sew them together. Most of the animal bodies can be sewn on a sewing machine, but you will need to hand sew gaps in the animals after you stuff them. Each project gives specific step-by-step instructions on how to sew the softies together. Wool felt is easy to sew with, as it's not slippery and it doesn't fray. So, it's the perfect material for beginners. If you prefer, you can also sew the entire animal by hand.

Tips for Successful Construction

- **The softies should all be sewn right sides together. Right side refers to the side that will be shown on the outside of the softie when it is finished. Even though I'm using a removable fabric marker, I use the side without any markings as the right side. So, the wrong side (the side with the pattern marks) faces out while you are sewing. This also helps me keep track of which side is which (since felt looks the same on both sides).**

- **The softies are irregularly shaped. When you need to switch directions while sewing, stop with the needle still in the fabric and lift the presser foot. Rotate the softie on the needle so that it is facing the direction you now need to stitch. Lower the presser foot, and continue sewing!**

- **The softies are sewn together in multiple stitching passes in order to correctly align all the pieces. Whenever you are connecting two different seams, overlap them by ¼˝ to ensure there are no gaps in the stitching.**

Stuffing the Softie

Stuffing a small softie can sometimes be trickier than it looks. A fundamental rule that makes this process easier is to only use small amounts of stuffing at a time. Fill each small corner of the animal piece by piece, only adding more stuffing once you've sufficiently filled one area. To achieve a well-defined animal shape, you need each nook and cranny, from head to toe, to be completely filled with stuffing. Use a dowel rod, chopstick, or the eraser end of a pencil to help with filling in tight areas. Each project has more detail about stuffing each animal shape.

Finishing

Threading the Needle and Finishing Stitches

The softies require lots of hand stitching to finish them nicely. Whether you're adding embroidery, faces and expressions, ears or tails, or just closing a gap, you'll need to stitch into their plush forms. When using six-stranded embroidery thread, separate to use just one strand.

Whenever you hand stitch, start by threading a hand-sewing needle with a piece of thread or floss about 25″-30″ long, bringing the two ends together so the length of thread is halved, and you're working with a double thread. Then, tie a double knot on the two loose ends of thread securing them together. Make the knot as close to the ends of the thread as possible.

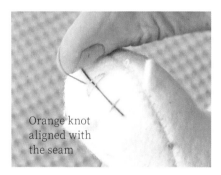

Orange knot aligned with the seam

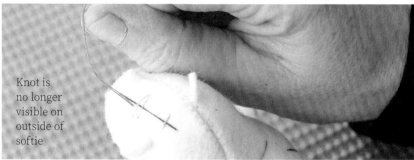

Knot is no longer visible on outside of softie

On the first stitch, pull the knotted thread flush with the softie. When possible, try to insert the first stitch through a seam on the animal.

Then, slightly tug on the thread, pulling the knot into the softie so it is no longer visible. If the stitch did not go through a seam, you may need to pull harder.

After stitching the final stitch, knot the thread flush to the softie. Thread the remaining tail onto the needle, then insert it into the softie next to the knot. Adjust the needle to exit the softie. Cut the tail flush with the felt; it may go inside the softie.

Whipstitch

A whipstitch is the hand-sewing stitch you need to close gaps after stuffing the softie, attach different parts like ears, or finish raw edges of fabric. It bridges the two pieces of fabric across the three-dimensional animal in a diagonal, visible stitch. With its versatility and simplicity, whipstitching ensures that your softies are well crafted and securely assembled.

1. Align the edges of the fabric pieces you're sewing together, such as the two pieces of fabric on either side of a gap. Insert the needle into one of the pieces of fabric from the back side, about ¼″ from the edge. Pull the needle through, securing the knot in the thread on the inside of the softie.

2. Pinch the two pieces of fabric together. Insert the needle through the front side of the opposite piece of fabric about ¼″ from the edge at a slight diagonal. Continue pushing the needle through and into the other piece of fabric, going from back to front until the needle pokes out the other side. Pull the needle and thread all the way through, creating a small visible stitch.

3. Repeat Step 2, creating small diagonal stitches that are very close together (less than ¼″ apart). The stitches don't need to be perfectly even or uniform, as the hand-stitched look gives your animal extra texture and personality.

Adding Ears, Horns, Fins, and Tails

All extra components outside of the animal's main body, like ears, horns, fins, and tails, will be sewn on after the softie is stuffed and sewn together.

Attaching Ears and Fins

1. Prepare the ear or fin as directed by the project. Pin the component to the softie as indicated by the pattern piece, or as you desire.

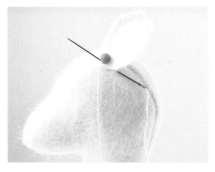  

2. Insert the threaded needle into the softie and back out through the component, securing the knotted thread beneath the component. Whipstitch the component securely to the softie.

Attaching Horns and Tails

Horns and tails need to be shaped into hollow tube-like pieces before they are stitched to the softie.

  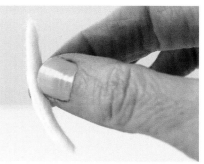

1. Hold the component pattern piece between your thumb and forefinger on one hand. Begin to roll the piece back and forth between your fingers, bringing the edges together.

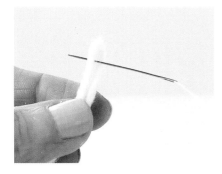  

2. Once you've created the shape indicated by the project, whipstitch the two edges of the tube together with small, close stitches. Follow the project instructions to create the specific shape needed for the animal.

3. Thread the needle again. Pin the component to the softie as indicated by the pattern piece, or as you desire.

4. Insert the needle into the softie and back out through the component, securing the knotted thread beneath the component. Whipstitch the component securely to the softie.

Adding Color

After taking great time and care to create your animal form, adding paint and color is just pure fun! Complete this step before adding final facial features or embroidery. For more on the painted designs and choosing colors, check out the Projects (page 24).

Set Up

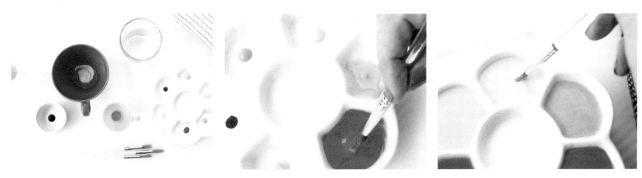

Gather your materials and set up a workspace. I suggest working in an area that you don't mind getting messy, or laying down a sheet of parchment paper or newsprint.

Select the colors of acrylic gouache you need, and squeeze out a small blob of paint in each color. Make sure each color has its own separate dish or palette section. Additionally, prepare a small spray bottle filled with water or rubbing alcohol, a hand towel, a cup of water, and a few medium round brushes. For more on these materials, see Tools and Materials (page 7).

Gently add drops of water to each color, mixing it with the paint. The ratio should be about 10 parts water to 1 part paint. Mix until the paint is completely dissolved.

Painting

1. Using the spray bottle, lightly mist the softie with the alcohol or water.

2. Dip a paintbrush into one of the diluted paints and apply it in a light swirl or organic blob over the softie. Repeat with a second color. Much like watercolor painting, the colors will begin to swirl and blend on the surface of the wool felt. Clean the brush between colors.

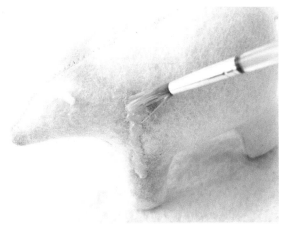

3. If you want more color to appear, put more paint onto the brush, and allow it to drip onto the softie. Take an abstract approach, adding and blending colors in random and unplanned ways. Continue until all the space is filled or you are happy with the result.

4. Let the softie dry completely. The colors will appear lighter when they are fully dried.

Crisper shapes on a dryer wool felt softie

Diluted marbling on a very wet wool felt softie

Tip

Experiment with the paint to water ratio. For brighter color, add more pigment, less water, and apply generously. Spray an area with more alcohol to dilute or blend colors together further. The wetter the softie is, the more the colors will bleed and blend, creating a soft marbled effect. Keep the surface dryer for crisper, more defined edges to the shapes you paint. If you make a mistake, use the spray bottle to wet the area well, diluting the color, and then try again.

Faces and Expressions

The face and expression you add to the softie is an important way to show the animal's unique personality! The eyes, nose, and mouth (as applicable) are marked on the pattern pieces. But, as your softie comes together, you may need to rethink or redraw the expression to best suit the finished animal. Start by using the fabric marking pen to draw the face details.

Eyes

I use acrylic gouache to paint on all of the eyes on my softies. It's a quick and easy alternative to stitching on the eyes.

1. Choose a dark color of acrylic gouache, like black or sepia. Dip the sharp end of a pin into the paint.

2. Align the pin with the marked eye. Insert the pin into the softie, pushing it in until all of the paint has transferred onto the felt. Repeat with the other eye. Let dry completely.

Nose and Mouth

I embroider the noses and mouths with small straight stitches and embroidery thread. When using six-stranded embroidery thread, separate to use just one strand doubled and knotted.

1. Insert the threaded needle at the top of the marked nose, going out the other side. Pull the needle through.

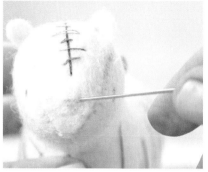
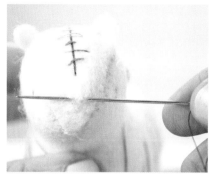
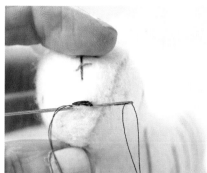

2. Repeat Step 1 just below the first stitch, stitching small, horizontal straight stitches that are progressively shorter and overlap with one another. This creates a triangle shape for the nose.

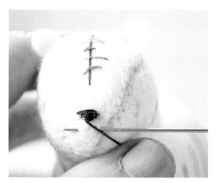

3. To stitch two intersecting diagonal lines for the mouth, insert the needle below the point of the nose, where you want one branch of the mouth to end. Push the needle through to the other side of the face, where you want the second branch to end. Finally, insert the needle back through the point of the nose, finishing the mouth.

Cheeks, Freckles, and Spots

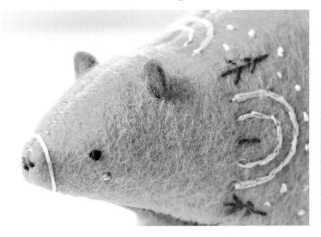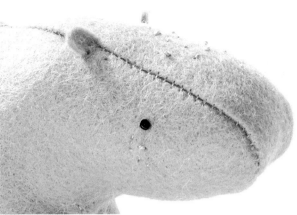

Using a series of tiny straight stitches will create small points of texture and character that are great for freckles and decorative embellishments.

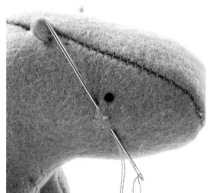

Add symmetrical dots on either side of a softie's face to create the impression of blush on their cheeks. Insert the needle on one side of the face, and bring it out on the other. Repeat moving in the opposite direction, inserting it and bringing it out right next to the original stitch.

Create small straight stitches for freckles by bringing the needle through the softie as tiny, close together intervals.

Embroidering Designs and Embellishments

You can mix-and-match any of the designs in the Embroidery Motif Library (page 22) with any of the animals. Follow the same basic steps in this section to stitch any of the designs. All embroidered designs are stitched onto the finished softies, but, if you prefer, you can also stitch them onto the flat pieces before you sew the softies together. I like embroidering after the softie is complete so I can envision the finished design better. When using six-stranded embroidery thread, separate to use just one strand.

Stitch Library

Use these three stitches to hand stitch all of the embroidery designs.

Straight Stitch

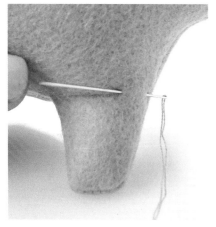 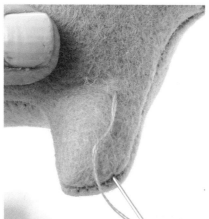 

1. Bring the threaded needle through the softie so it comes out at the starting point of the stitch.

2. Insert the needle back through the softie at the desired stitch end point. In the example pictured, insert the needle through the bottom of the foot. Then, continue pushing the needle through so that it emerges at the start point of the next stitch.

3. Repeat Steps 1–2 to continue stitching, keeping the stitches straight and even length.

Chain Stitch

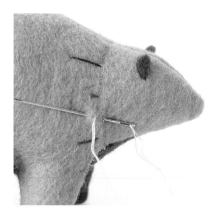 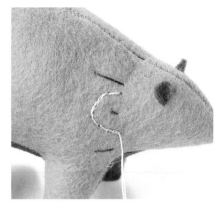 

1. Push the threaded needle through the softie, parallel with the surface, where the first stitch should be. Pull the needle and thread through, leaving some slack in the thread. Separate the double strand of thread against the softie.

2. Doubling back, insert the needle through the gap between the double strand of thread. Push the needle back out where the second stitch should end. Again, leave some slack in the thread, and separate the double strand of thread.

3. Repeat Steps 1–2 to create connected chain stitches. Space the stitches evenly.

Seed Stitch

1. Push the threaded needle through the softie, parallel with the surface, to create a small straight stitch. Repeat this process, creating small straight stitches randomly or as indicated by the instructions across the area. Make the stitches evenly spaced and slightly varied in length.

Embroidery Motif Library

Check out Templates (page 122) for the full-size templates of each motif that you can trace onto the softies. This chapter gives you a short visual breakdown of how to stitch each design. There are a few embroidery motifs included that are not shown on the finished softies. Feel free to swap and mix-and-match the designs as you prefer!

SWEEPING CORAL BRANCH

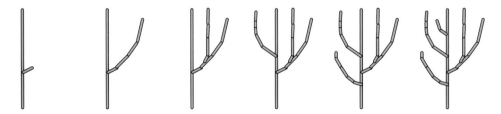

FRINGED CORAL BRANCH

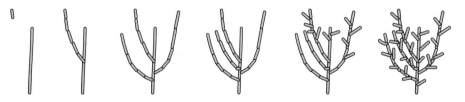

ANEMONE CORAL

STAR CORAL

SPIRAL CORAL

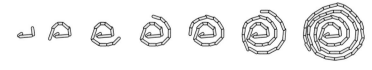

PINE TREE

MINI RAINBOW

THISTLE

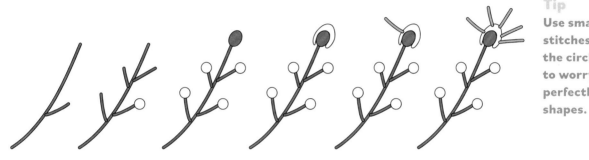

Tip
Use small straight stitches to stitch the circles; no need to worry about perfectly round shapes.

BERRIES

MUSHROOM

ASTER

DANDELION

BRANCH

Projects

Stitch all projects with a ¼″ seam allowance. Be sure to review the information in Basic Techniques (page 10), as these instructions give additional information needed for making every softie project.

Simple Elephant

Trunks up if you love elephants! These ones are the perfect size for holding in your hand. Choose a natural shade as pictured here, or sew a pink elephant parade. This is a wonderfully simple project that's excellent for beginners and the perfect place to start your softie party.

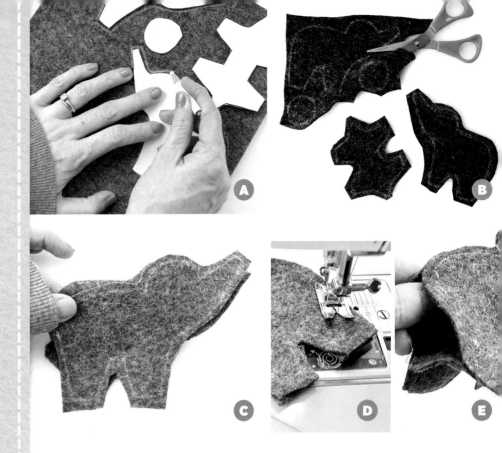

Materials

8″ × 12″ sheet of merino wool felt in dark gray (or color of your choice)

Scissors

Fabric pen or pencil

Sewing machine

Matching all-purpose sewing thread

Hand-sewing needle

Sewing pins

Polyfill stuffing

Dowel rod (or similar tool, like a chopstick)

Acrylic gouache in black

Simple Elephant templates (page 123)

TEMPLATES

Before beginning the project, print or trace the needed templates onto paper or cardstock. For this project, you need Simple Elephant Templates A–D.

Cut & Sew

1. Trace the templates onto the felt sheet with the fabric pencil. Trace 2 of Template D. Be sure to transfer over all pattern marks. Cut out the felt pieces. **A-B**

2. Layer piece A over piece C, right sides together and matching dots and *X*s. The tip of piece C should line up with the neck and chest of piece A. Pin if needed. Starting at the tip of piece C on the chest, sew all the way to the mark at the top of the back leg. **C**

3. Flip over the unit from Step 2. Fold piece C in half toward the bottom of the elephant, then layer piece B on top (right sides together), lining up the legs and chest. Sew piece B and piece C together, starting at the mark at the top of the back leg and sewing to the end of piece C. **D**

4. Sew pieces A and B together. Start at the triangle above the butt, and sew together the back, head, and trunk, stopping after slightly overlapping the stitching from Steps 2 and 3. The only remaining gap in the elephant should be at the butt. **E**

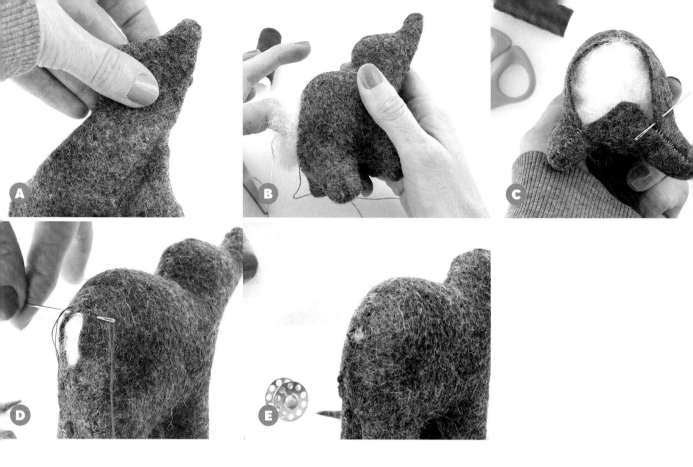

Stuff the Softie

1. Turn the elephant right side out, poking out all the edges, corners, and points with the dowel rod. **A**

2. Stuff the body with polyfill. Pack it firmly, starting at the tip of the trunk and working your way toward the opening until the form is well stuffed. Make sure to press stuffing into each leg. **B**

3. Hand sew the opening at the back of the elephant with a whipstitch (page 13), tucking in the raw edges. Start from the bottom of the opening and work upward, sewing each leg separately. Add stuffing as you sew to fill out the form completely. You want the elephant to be round and plush. Once the legs are stitched closed, finally, whipstitch the remaining gap closed. **C-E**

Note
At this stage, you may notice small gaps in the stitching around the elephant, as a stitch or 2 may pop while you're turning and stuffing the elephant. Hand stitch any little gaps closed now.

Add the Details

1. To make the tail, roll the E piece between your fingers and stitch the edges with a whipstitch (see Attaching Horns and Tails, page 14). Pin both D pieces, the ears, and the tail in place as marked on the pattern, or adjust them as you prefer. Whipstitch onto the softie. **A-B**

2. Dip the tip of a pin into the black paint. Slowly and carefully, poke the painted end of the pin into the softie where the eye is marked. Slowly remove it. Repeat on the other eye. Let dry completely before touching to avoid smudging. **C-E**

Dream Whale

This wee baby blue whale is having quite a splash!
The spacey, dreamy details are created with paint and
embroidery thread, making this whale cuddly and
magical enough to bring anyone sweet dreams.

Materials

8″ × 12″ sheets of merino wool felt in navy and tan

Scissors

Fabric pen or pencil

Sewing machine

Matching all-purpose sewing thread

Hand-sewing needle

Embroidery floss in purple and aqua

Sewing pins

Polyfill stuffing

Dowel rod (or similar tool)

Acrylic gouache in light blue and lilac

Spray bottle with rubbing alcohol or water

Round paint brushes (1–2)

Small cups or palette for mixing paint (one per color)

Hand towel or paper towel

Dream Whale templates (page 124)

TEMPLATES

Before beginning your project, print or trace the needed templates onto paper or cardstock. For this project, you need Dream Whale Templates A–E.

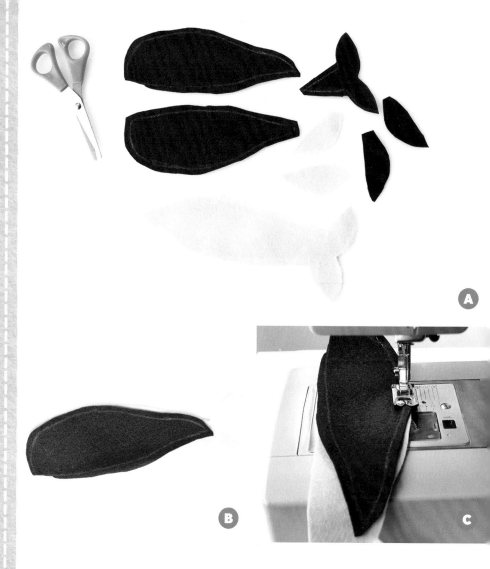

Cut & Sew

1. Trace the templates onto the felt sheets with the fabric pen. Transfer 2 piece Es to tan felt, and 2 piece Es to navy fabric. Transfer piece C to tan felt, and pieces A, B, and D to navy felt. Be sure to transfer over all pattern marks. Cut out the felt pieces. **A**

2. Layer pieces A and C together as shown, right sides together and matching dots and Xs. Pin if needed. Sew along the bottom of the whale, from the mark on the nose to the mark at the base of the tail. **B-C**

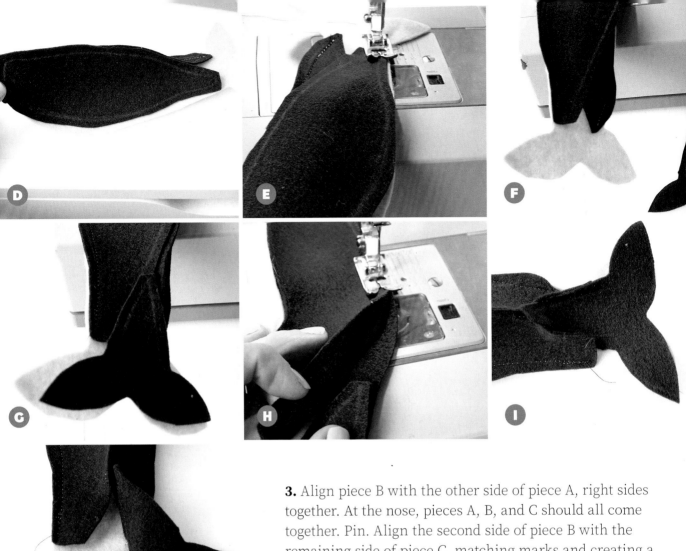

3. Align piece B with the other side of piece A, right sides together. At the nose, pieces A, B, and C should all come together. Pin. Align the second side of piece B with the remaining side of piece C, matching marks and creating a triangle-like tube. Pin. Sew together pieces B and C from the base of the tail to the nose mark, keeping piece A out of the way until you reach the nose. At the nose, stitch over piece A, joining the 3 pieces together. Stop with the needle at this intersection point. **D-F**

4. Rotate the whale on the machine, turning so you can begin to stitch pieces A and B together (without stitching piece C). Before you start stitching, align piece D with piece A, right sides together. Align the tail shape with piece C. Begin stitching again, attaching pieces A and B. When you reach piece D, lift piece B out of the way, stitching only pieces A and D together. Continue to the end of piece A. **G-J**

K

L

5. Layer the E pieces together with the navy on top and tan on the bottom, making 2 pairs. **K**

6. Sew around the shape of the fin, leaving the straight, short end unsewn. **L**

Stuff the Softie

1. Turn the whale right side out, poking out all the edges, corners, and points with the dowel rod. **A-B**

2. Stuff the body with polyfill. Pack it firmly, starting at the head and working your way toward the opening, until the form is well stuffed. **C-D**

A

B

C

D

3. Once the body is well stuffed, begin hand sewing the opening closed with the navy sewing thread. Starting at the whale's back and moving down the tail, whipstitch (page 13) the gap closed using a Y-shaped seam. Tuck in the raw edges. Add more stuffing while you stitch as needed to make the whale plush. Stop once you reach the fins. **E-G**

Add the Details

Attach the Fins

1. Pin the fins to the body where marked on the pattern or as desired. **A-B**

2. With the navy thread, whipstitch the fins to the body. **C-D**

Add Color

For this particular project, the painting results in a semi-opaque wash. The paint should be diluted at a ratio of about 1 drop of paint to 20 drops of water. A little dab of paint will go a long way. Once applied, if the color is too light, add a small bit more paint to the mixture. For more color tips, see Adding Color (page 15).

1. Dilute the light blue and lilac paint in separate cups or palette bowls. Be sure to mix well, taking time to dissolve all the paint with the brush. **E**

2. Mist the whale's body with the spray bottle filled with rubbing alcohol or water. Small droplets will be visible on the felt. **F**

3. Dip the brush into one paint color, and lightly press it against the whale. As soon as the paint makes contact with the material, the color will run and blend as it's being absorbed by the wool. **G-H**

4. Continue adding patches of color all over the navy felt of the whale. Try layering colors over one other and misting areas to create more blending effects. When the paint dries, the colors will be much lighter than they appeared when wet. You may want to apply the colors a second time. **I-L**

Add the Embroidery

1. Mark the eye placement with pins. **M**

2. Insert the hand-sewing needle threaded with black thread. Go in near the base of the head, and out at the eye point. Use layered straight stitches (page 20) to stitch an almond shape for the eye. Repeat on the opposite side of the face. **N-O**

3. With the purple embroidery floss, stitch the mouth onto the whale with a chain stitch (page 21) or straight stitch (page 20). Follow the guide on the pattern pieces, or freehand draw the mouth with the fabric pen before stitching. **P-T**

4. With the aqua embroidery floss, add a few seed stitches (page 21) around the eyes. Follow the guide on the pattern pieces, or freehand the design. **U**

5. Finally, align the whale's tail pieces. Sew the tails closed by following the outline with the sewing machine. **V-W**

Tip
If you prefer, you can sew the tails closed (Step 5 above) before painting the whale instead of leaving it until the end.

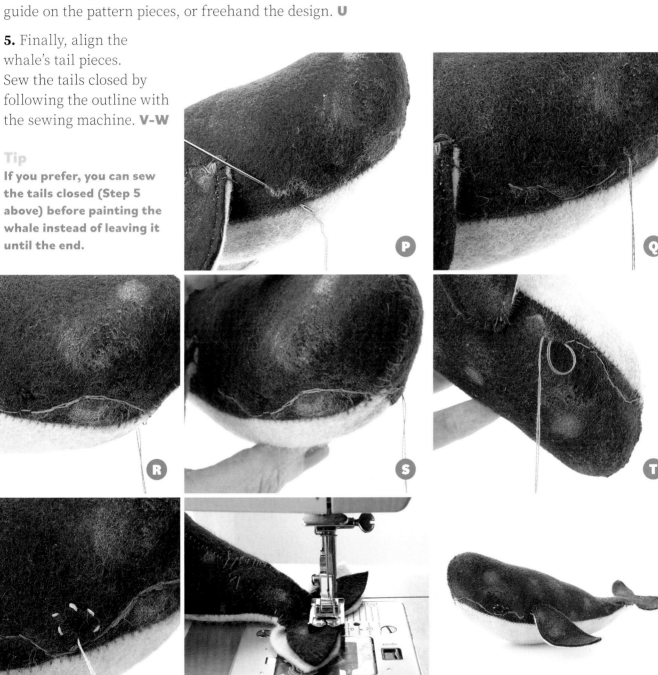

Rainbow Tiger

What could be more fierce than a tiger? Why only a rainbow tiger, of course! Sew up and squeeze this softie when you need to be brave. The color combinations between the felt and the stripes are endless!

Materials

8″ × 12″ sheet of merino wool felt in white

Scissors

Fabric pen or pencil

Sewing machine

All-purpose sewing thread in white

Hand-sewing needle

Embroidery floss in navy, lilac, orange, and aqua

Sewing pins

Polyfill stuffing

Dowel rod (or similar tool, like a chopstick)

Acrylic gouache in black

Rainbow Tiger templates (pages 125–126)

TEMPLATES

Before beginning the project, print or trace the needed templates onto paper or cardstock. For this project, you need Rainbow Tiger Templates A–F.

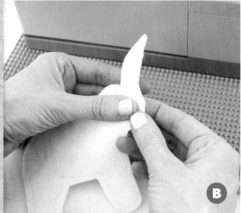

Cut & Sew

1. Trace the templates onto the felt sheet with the fabric pen. Trace 2 of Template E. Be sure to transfer over all pattern marks. Cut out the felt pieces. **A**

2. Layer pieces A and D right sides together, matching the star of piece D with the star on the piece A chin. Sew together. **B-C**

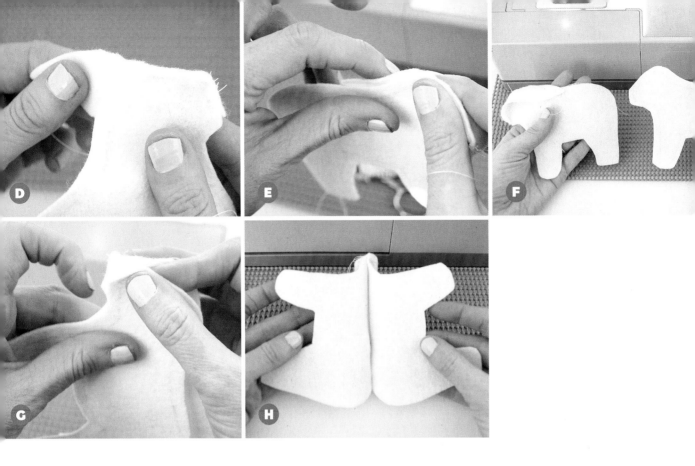

3. Pull down the long top edge of piece D, aligning it with the top edge of piece A. The dot on piece D should align with the dot at the center back. Pin if needed. Sew together, starting at the center back dot and stitching toward the snout. **D-E**

4. Lift up the flap of piece D and align it with the snout and top edge of piece B, right sides together. The star of piece D and the snout points on pieces A and B should all meet. Pin if needed, keeping piece A out of the way. **F-G**

5. Starting from the tip of the snout, sew piece B to piece D until you reach the end of piece D. Then, align pieces A and B, and continue sewing A and B together to the back mark just above the butt. **H**

6. Pull pieces A and B apart, then sandwich piece C between them, aligning all 4 legs right sides together. Sew piece A to piece C from the dot at the top of the back leg to the snout point at the base of the chin, overlapping the existing stitching slightly. At the chest, align one edge of the piece C tip with piece A and continue sewing. Do not sew through piece B when attaching pieces A and C.

Repeat on the other side, attaching pieces B and C from the *X* at the back leg to the chin. Do not sew through piece A when attaching pieces B and C. **I-J**

Stuff the Softie

1. Turn the tiger right side out, poking out all the edges, corners, and points with the dowel rod. **A**

2. Stuff the body with polyfill. Pack it firmly, starting at the tip of the nose and working your way toward the opening until the form is well stuffed. Make sure to press stuffing into each leg. **B**

3. Begin sewing up the back side. Start by whipstitching (page 13) from the bottom of the gap on one leg to the base of the butt. Tuck in the raw edges. Repeat on the other back leg. Add more stuffing as you stitch to continue to fill out the body. **C-D**

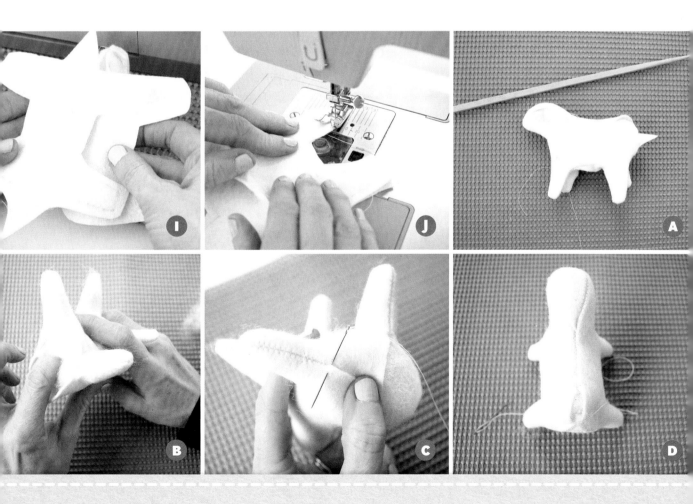

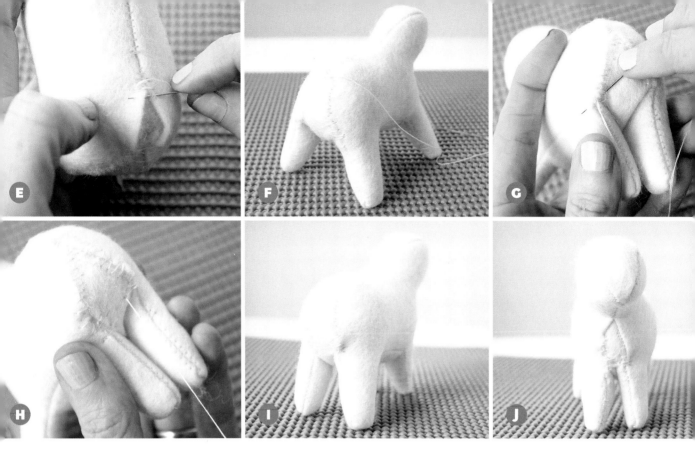

4. Whipstitch the remaining gap closed, again adding more stuffing as you go. Tuck in the raw edges. **E-F**

5. Add some additional stitches to improve the structure of the softie. Pinch the back legs together as shown. Add a couple of whipstitches on the creases formed, holding the legs closer to the body so the softie stands straighter. Repeat on the front legs. **G-J**

Add the Details

Attach the Ears and Tail

1. Pin both E pieces, the ears, in place as marked on the pattern, or adjust them as you prefer. **A**

2. To make the tail, roll the F piece between your fingers and stitch the edges with a whipstitch (see Attaching Horns and Tails, page 14). Pin the tail to the top of the butt, or adjust it as you prefer. **B**

3. Hand sew the flat edge of each ear to the body with a whipstitch.

4. Hand sew the flat edge of the tail to the body with a whipstitch. **C**

Add the Embroidery

For more on embroidering the softies, see Embroidering Designs and Embellishments (page 20).

1. Starting with the navy embroidery floss, stitch a series of long, vertical straight stitches spaced out over the tiger's body. Follow the pattern if desired, or stitch as you prefer. Leave space between the stripes for other colors to fill in. Vary the length and placement (start/end points) of the stripes. **D-E**

2. Using the lilac embroidery floss, stitch some horizontal straight stitches that cross the navy lines, as shown on the pattern. Then, add lilac vertical stripes between the navy stripes. **F**

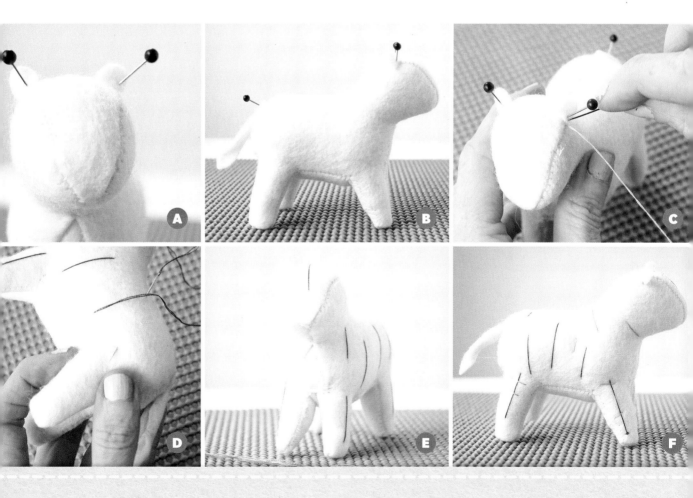

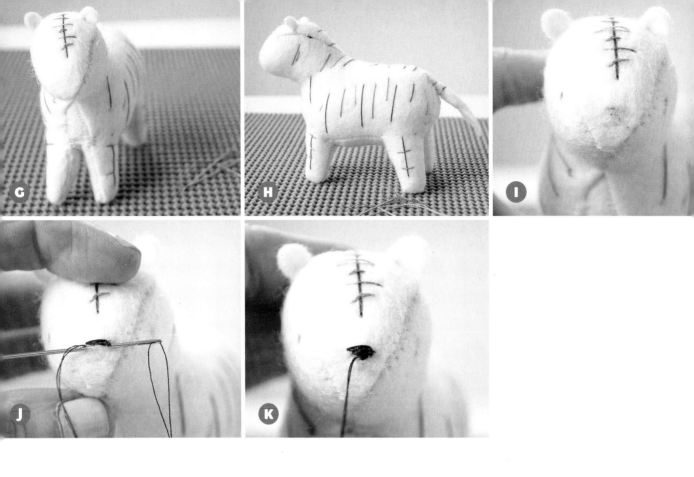

3. Repeat Step 2 with the orange and aqua floss, filling in stripes (both vertical and horizontal) across the tiger's body. **G-H**

Add the Face

1. With the fabric marker, draw the eyes, nose, and mouth as shown on the pattern. **I**

2. Using the navy floss, insert the needle at the top of the marked nose, going out the other side. Pull the needle through. Repeat the process, stitching small, horizontal straight stitches that are progressively shorter and overlap with one another to create a triangle shape for the nose. **J-K**

3. To stitch 2 intersecting diagonal lines for the mouth, insert the needle below the point of the nose, where you want one branch of the mouth to end. Push the needle through to the other side of the face, where you want the second branch to end. Finally, insert the needle back through the point of the nose, finishing the mouth. Tie a double knot at the top of the mouth, then trim the thread tail flush. **L-P**

4. Dip the tip of a pin into the black paint. Slowly and carefully, poke the painted end of the pin into the softie where the eye is marked. Slowly remove it. Repeat on the other eye. Let dry completely before touching to avoid smudging. **Q-S**

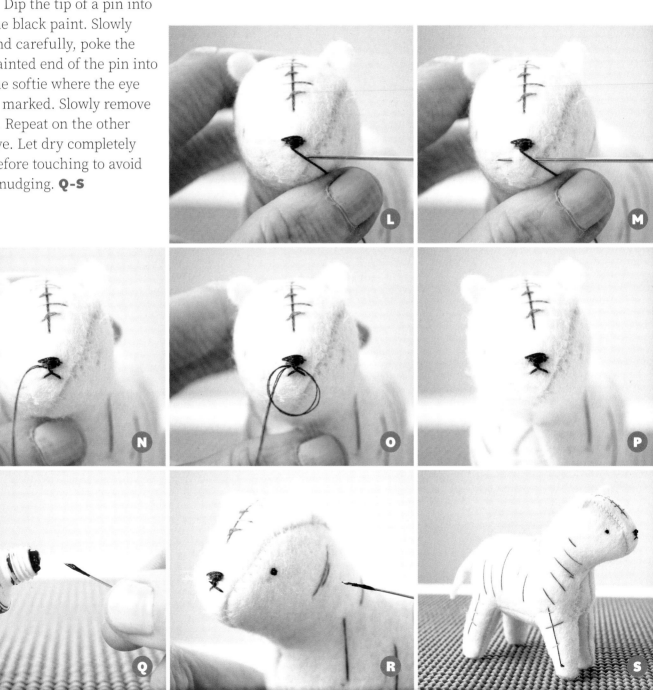

White Bison

White bison are sacred animals to many First Nation Native American people. These animals are viewed as harbingers of hope, rebirth, peace, and unity.

Materials

8″ × 12″ sheets of merino wool felt in white

6″ × 3″ piece of viscose fur in white

Scissors

Fabric pen or pencil

Sewing machine

All-purpose sewing thread in white and pale yellow

Hand-sewing needle

Embroidery floss in black

Sewing pins

Polyfill stuffing

Dowel rod (or similar tool)

Acrylic gouache in yellow and black

Spray bottle with rubbing alcohol or water

Round paint brushes

Small cups or palette for mixing paint into (one per color)

Hand towel or paper towel

White Bison templates (pages 127–128)

TEMPLATES

Before beginning the project, print or trace the needed templates onto paper or cardstock. For this project, you need White Bison Templates A–H.

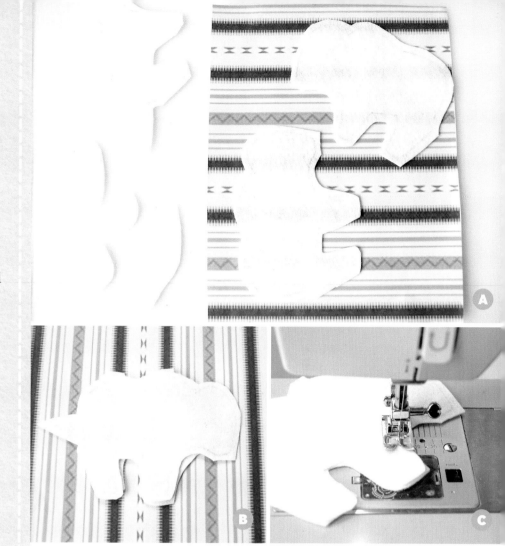

Cut & Sew

1. Trace the templates onto the felt sheet with the fabric pen. Trace 4 of piece E. Trace pieces G and H onto the viscose fur instead of the felt. Be sure to transfer over all pattern marks. Cut out the felt pieces. **A**

2. Layer piece A over piece C, right sides together. The longer leg on piece C should align with the front leg on piece A. The star of piece C should line up with the star of piece A. Pin if needed. **B**

3. Starting at the star at the chin, sew all the way to the dot at the top of the back leg. **C**

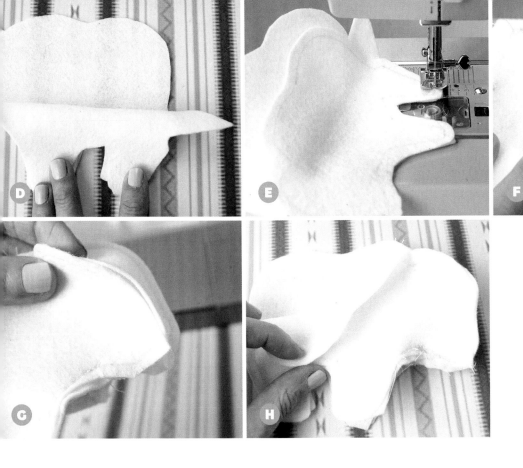

4. Flip over the unit from Step 3. Fold piece C in half toward the bottom of the bison, then layer piece B on top (right sides together), lining up the legs and chest. Sew piece B and piece C together, starting at the mark at the top of the back leg and sewing to the star at the chin. Do not sew through piece A. **D-E**

5. Align the star on the point of piece D with the star on the chin of piece B, right sides together. Starting at the chin, stitch the two pieces together to the triangle at the back of the neck. **F**

6. Repeat Step 5 to sew piece D to piece A. Pinch piece D in half so they are aligned right sides together. **G**

7. Sew pieces A and B together along the back of the bison starting at the neck, slightly overlapping the existing stitches. Stop stitching at the mark above the butt, leaving a gap for stuffing. **H**

Stuff the Softie

1. Turn the bison right side out, poking out all the edges, corners, and points with the dowel rod. **I-J**

2. Stuff the body with polyfill. Pack it firmly, starting at the tip of the nose and working your way toward the opening until the form is well stuffed. Make sure to press stuffing into each leg. **K-L**

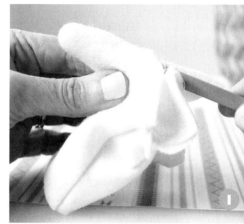

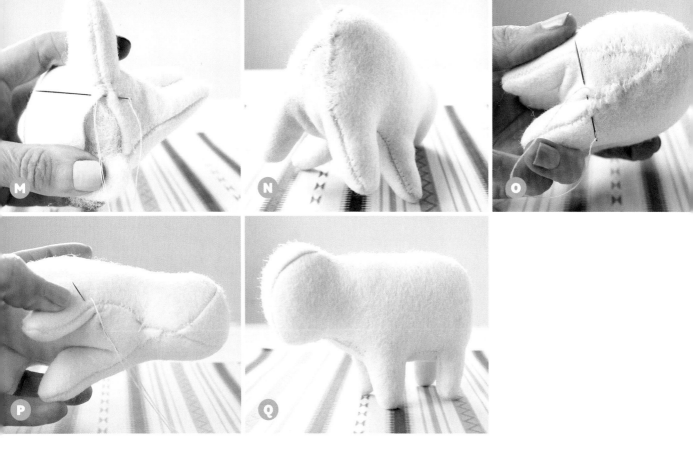

3. Begin sewing up the back side. Start by whipstitching (page 13) from the bottom of the gap on one leg to the base of the butt. Tuck in the raw edges. Repeat on the other back leg. Add more stuffing as you stitch to continue to fill out the body. **M**

4. Whipstitch the remaining gap closed, again adding more stuffing as you go. Tuck in the raw edges. **N**

5. Add some additional stitches to improve the structure of the softie. Pinch the back legs together as shown. Add a couple of whipstitches on the creases formed, holding the legs closer to the body so the softie stands straighter. Repeat on the front legs. **O-Q**

Add the Fur

1. Cut pieces G and H out of the fur.

2. Drape piece G over the back of the bison as shown and as marked on the pattern. **A**

3. Overlap the points of piece G on the bison's chest, and pin. Tuck in the raw edges around the front of the fur, and pin. **B-C**

4. With the hand-sewing needle threaded with white thread, insert the needle at the intersection of piece G. Whipstitch the 2 edges together securely. **D-E**

5. Stitch the rest of the fur to the softie with straight stitches (page 20) around the whole shape. Make each stitch about ½″ apart. **F**

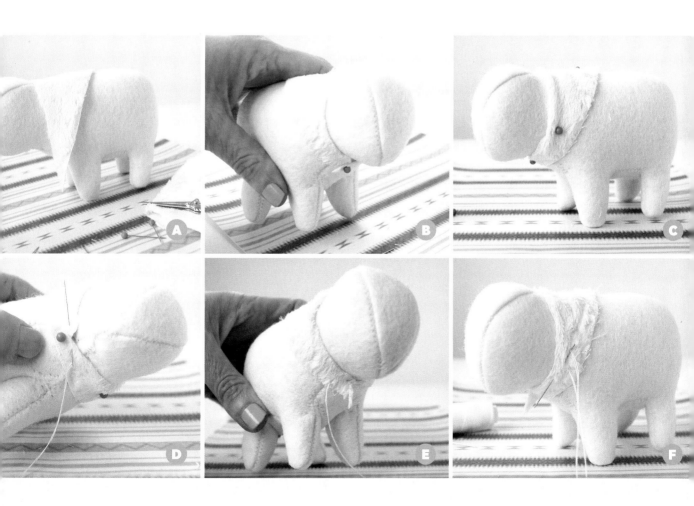

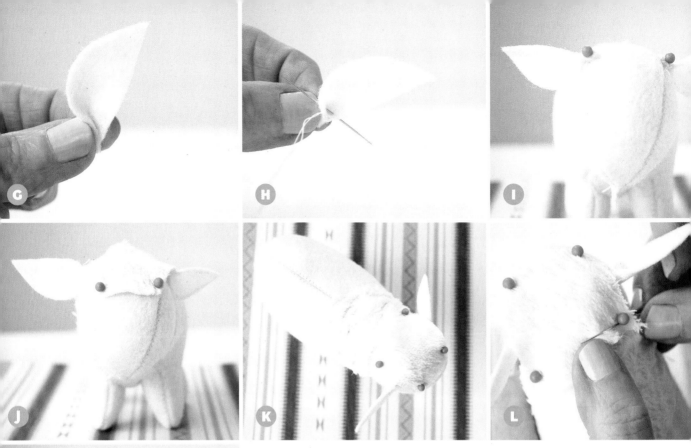

Attach the Ears

1. Pinch the bottom edge of each ear. Secure the fold with a few whipstitches. **G-H**

2. Pin them to the top of the head as shown, or as marked on the pattern. Whipstitch the ears to the head. **I**

3. Pin piece H to the top of the head as shown. **J-K**

4. Starting behind 1 ear, whipstitch all the way around the raw edges of piece H, attaching it to the bison. **L-M**

Attach the Tail

1. Prepare piece F, the tail, by following the instructions in Attaching Horns and Tails (page 14). **N**

2. Pin the tail to the top of the butt. Whipstitch the tail to the softie. **O**

Attach the Horns

1. Prepare the remaining 2 E pieces, the horns, by following the instructions in Attaching Horns and Tails (page 14). Shape them to a point on both ends. **P**

2. Pin the horns to the head just above the ears, as shown. Whipstitch the horns to the head. **Q-R**

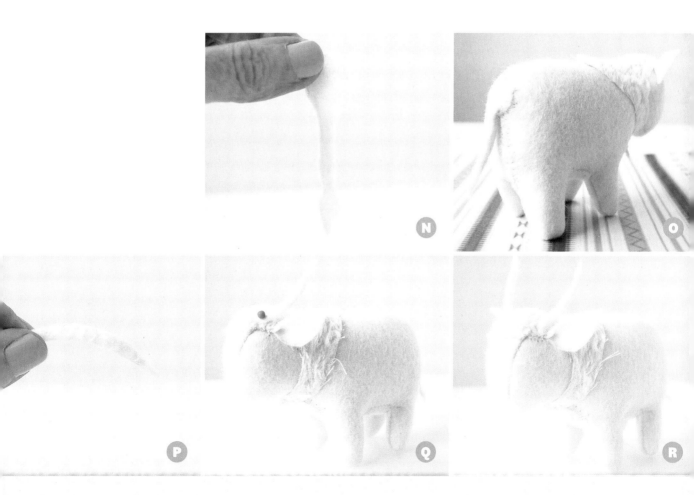

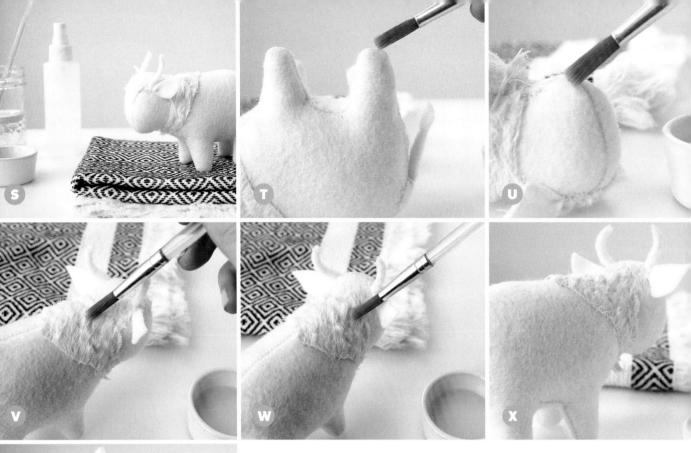

Add Color

For this particular project, the desired painted effect is a semi-opaque paint wash. The paint should be diluted at a ratio of about 1 drop of paint to 20 drops of water. A little dab of paint will go a long way. Once applied, if the color is too light add a small bit more paint to the mixture. For more color mixing tips, see Adding Color (page 15).

1. Mix up a wash with the yellow acrylic gouache paint. Be sure to mix well, taking time to dissolve all the paint with the brush. Mist the body with the spray bottle filled with rubbing alcohol or water. Small droplets will be visible on the material. **S**

2. Flip the bison on its back. Dip the brush into the paint mixture and lightly press it against the bottom of each foot. Then, press it on the tip of the snout/nose. Let dry slightly. **T-U**

3. Turn the bison over and spray the fur collar and head. Apply paint to the fur, coloring it completely. Add a dab of yellow to the tip of the tail. Add a very light wash to the bison's face. Let dry completely. If the colors look too light after they dry, reapply. **V-Y**

Add the Face

1. Use the fabric marker to mark the eyes and the nose from the pattern. **Z**

2. Using the black thread, insert the needle at the top of the marked nose, going out the other side. Pull the needle through. Repeat the process, stitching small, horizontal straight stitches that are progressively shorter and overlap with one another to create a triangle shape for the nose. **A-C**

3. Dip the tip of a pin into the black paint. Slowly and carefully, poke the painted end of the pin into the softie where the eye is marked. Slowly remove it. Repeat on the other eye. Let dry completely before touching to avoid smudging. **D-E**

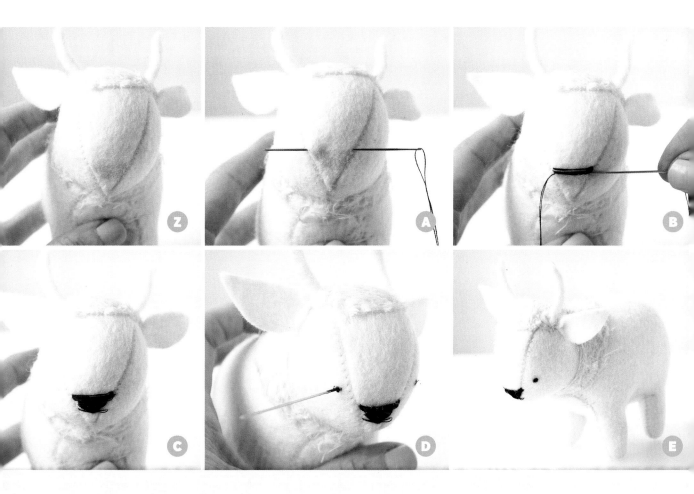

Cloud Bear

Cloud bears are a fun exploration of abstract and unique felt painting. Mix your own colors to create one-of-a-kind bears that look like they should be wandering through cotton candy clouds at sunset.

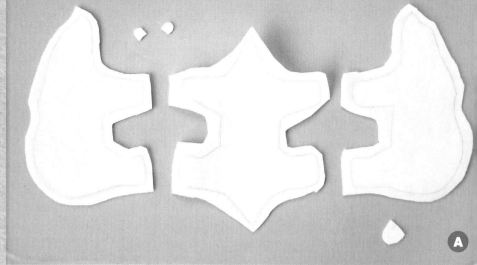

Materials

8″ × 12″ sheet of merino wool felt in white

Scissors

Fabric pen or pencil

Sewing machine

Matching all-purpose sewing thread

Hand-sewing needle

Embroidery floss in aqua

Sewing pins

Polyfill stuffing

Dowel rod (or similar tool)

Acrylic gouache in black

6 colors of acrylic gouache for the body (orange, lilac, light blue, rose, shell pink, and flesh)

Spray bottle with rubbing alcohol or water

Round paint brushes

Small cups or palette for mixing paint (one per color)

Hand towel or paper towel

Bear templates (page 143)

TEMPLATES

Before beginning the project, print or trace the needed templates onto paper or cardstock. For this project, you need Bear Templates A–E.

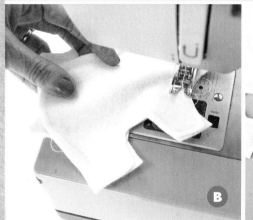

Cut & Sew

1. Trace the templates onto the felt sheet with the fabric pen. Trace 2 of piece E. Be sure to transfer over all pattern marks. Cut out the felt pieces. **A**

2. Layer piece A over piece C, right sides together and matching dots and Xs. The tip of piece C should line up with the neck and chest of piece A. Pin if needed. Starting at the tip of piece C on the chest, sew all the way to the mark at the top of the back leg. **B**

3. Flip over the unit from Step 2. Fold piece C in half toward the bottom of the bear, then layer piece B on top (right sides together), lining up the legs and chest. Sew piece B and piece C together, starting at the mark at the top of the back leg and sewing to the end of piece C. **C**

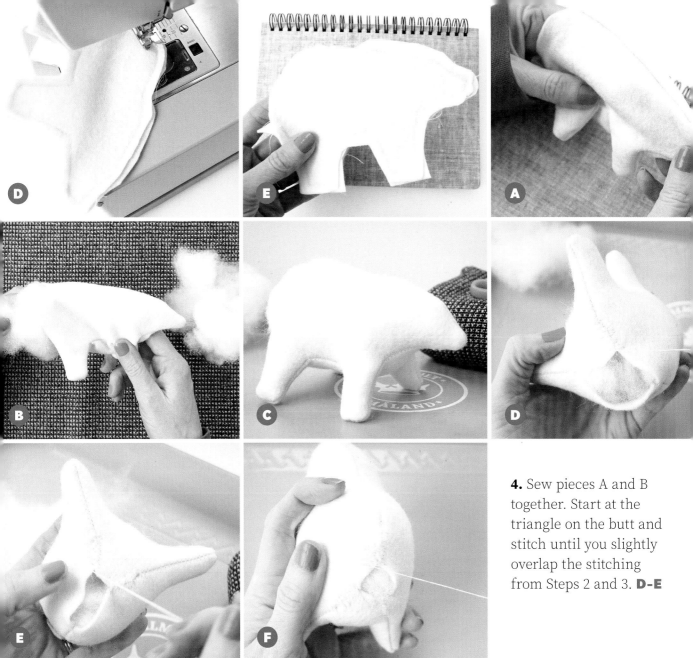

Stuff the Softie

1. Turn the bear right side out, poking out all the edges, corners, and points with the dowel rod. **A**

2. Stuff the body with polyfill. Pack it firmly, starting at the tip of the nose and working your way toward the opening until the form is well stuffed. Make sure to press stuffing into each leg. **B-C**

3. Hand sew the opening at the back of the bear with a whipstitch (page 13), tucking in the raw edges. Start from the bottom of the opening and work upward, sewing each leg separately. Add stuffing as you sew to fill out the form completely. You want the bear to be round and plush. Once the legs are closed stitched together, finally, whipstitch the remaining gap closed. **D-F**

4. Add some additional stitches to improve the structure of the softie. Pinch the back legs together as shown. Add a couple of whipstitches on the creases formed, holding the legs closer to the body so the softie stands straighter. Repeat on the front legs. **G-I**

Add the Details

1. Pin both D pieces, the ears, in place as marked on the pattern or as you prefer. Repeat with piece F, the tail. **A**

2. Whipstitch the flat edge of each ear to the body. Repeat with the tail. **B**

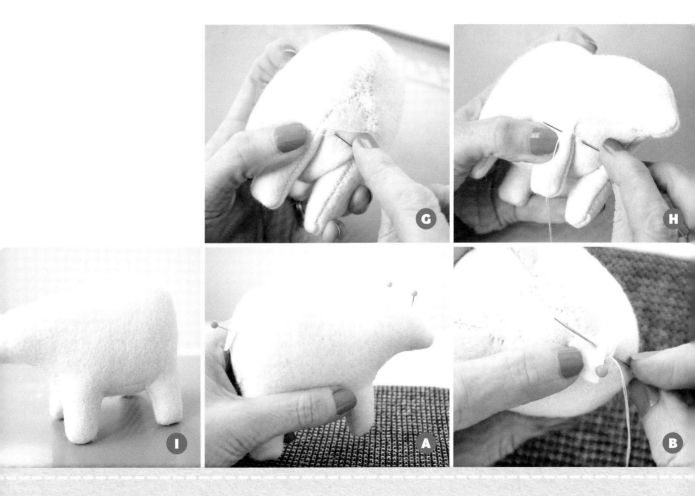

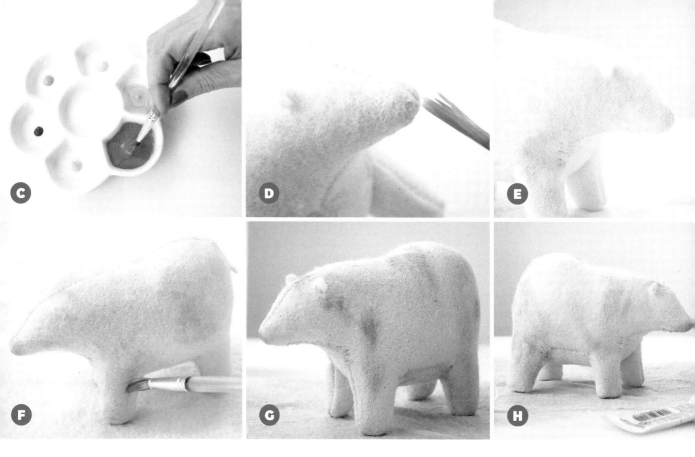

Add Color

For this project the desired painted effect is a soft pastel wash. The paint should be diluted at a ratio of about 1 drop of paint to 20 drops of water. A little dab of paint will go a long way. Once applied, if the color is too light, add a small bit more paint to the mixture. For more color mixing tips, see Adding Color (page 15).

1. Dilute all 6 colors of paint in separate containers. Though you may not use all 6 colors, I prefer having them all available. **C**

2. Mist the bear with the spray bottle filled with rubbing alcohol or water. Small droplets will be visible on the material. Dip the brush into the paint mixture and lightly press it against the felt. I often start with the bear's muzzle and work across the body. As soon as the paint makes contact with the material, the color will run and blend as it's being absorbed by the wool. **D**

3. Continue adding dabs of color all over the bear's body. Experiment by layering different colors on top of one another. As the bear begins to dry, spray it again. **E-F**

4. Once all the white space has been covered and the colors dry lighter, you may want to add more layers of color for brighter highlights across the body. After adding the final layer, set the bear aside to dry completely. **G-H**

Add the Face

1. Mark the nose and eyes with the fabric pen, as shown on the template. Thread the hand-sewing needle with the aqua embroidery floss. Insert the needle through the bear's snout (on the seam line). **I-J**

2. Begin embroidering the bear's nose. Stitch overlapping horizontal straight stitches (see Nose and Mouth, page 18). Stitch a small triangle, then tie a knot flush with the felt. **K**

3. Dip the tip of a pin into the black paint. Slowly and carefully, poke the painted end of the pin into the softie where the eye is marked. Slowly remove it. Repeat on the other eye. Let dry completely before touching to avoid smudging. **L-M**

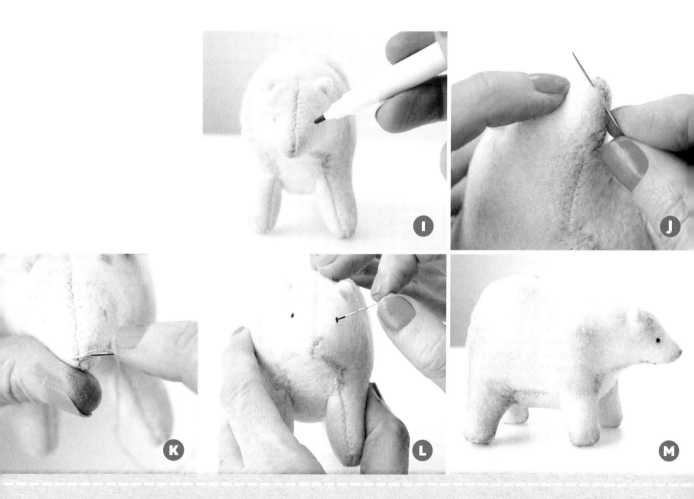

Baby Brontosaurus

Baby dinosaurs are the very best pets to have. They are sweet and small and eat all the vegetables you don't want to finish!

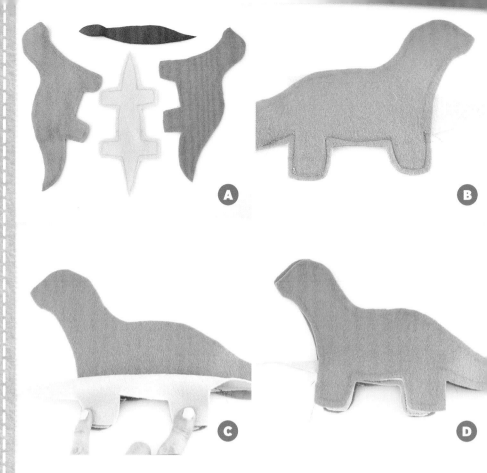

Materials

8″ × 12″ sheets of merino wool felt in moss green, peach, and spruce green

Scissors

Fabric pen or pencil

Sewing machine

All-purpose sewing thread in green

Hand-sewing needle

Embroidery floss in bright orange

Sewing pins

Polyfill stuffing

Dowel rod (or similar tool)

Acrylic gouache in black

Baby Brontosaurus templates (pages 128–129)

TEMPLATES

Before beginning the project, print or trace the needed templates onto paper or cardstock. For this project, you need Baby Brontosaurus Templates A, B, and C.

Cut & Sew

1. Trace the templates onto the felt sheets with the fabric pencil. Trace 2 of Template A, flipping the template over to trace the second. Transfer both A pieces to the moss green felt, B to the peach felt, and C to the spruce green felt. Be sure to transfer over all pattern marks. Cut out the felt pieces. **A**

2. Align B with a piece A, right sides together, and with the one side of the feet matched up. Sew from the dot at the top of the front leg to the dot on the tail. **B**

3. Fold piece B in half, bringing the other set of feet down. Place the other piece A on top, right sides together, and matching up the feet again. Repeat Step 2 to sew together. **C-D**

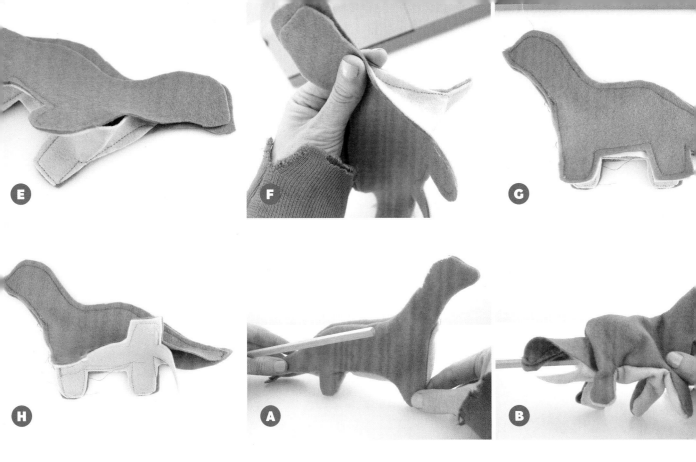

4. Overlapping the stitching from Step 3 slightly, stitch one side of the neck to piece B. Stitch until the *X*. **E**

5. Flip the dinosaur over, and repeat Step 4, closing the gap in the neck. Instead of stopping at the *X*, continue stitching both A pieces together. Sew over the head and down the back and tail. Stop just past the end point of the tail. Do not sew through piece B when stitching the tail. **F-H**

Stuff the Softie

1. Turn the dinosaur right side out, poking out all the edges, corners, and points with the dowel rod. **A**

2. Stuff the body with polyfill. Pack it firmly, starting at the tip of the nose and working your way toward the opening until the form is well stuffed. Make sure to press stuffing into each leg. **B**

3. Hand sew the opening at the back of the tail with a whipstitch (page 13) and green thread, tucking in the raw edges. Start at one leg and continue to the point of the tail. Add stuffing as you sew to fill out the form completely. Repeat on the other leg and side of the tail. As you move up the tail, completely enclose piece B, leaving just a small tube open. **C-D**

4. Stuff the tail with the dowel rod. Then, whipstitch up to the point of the tail. **E-G**

5. Add some additional stitches to improve the structure of the softie. Pinch the back legs together as shown. Add a couple of whipstitches on the creases formed, holding the legs closer to the body so the softie stands straighter. Repeat on the front legs. **H-I**

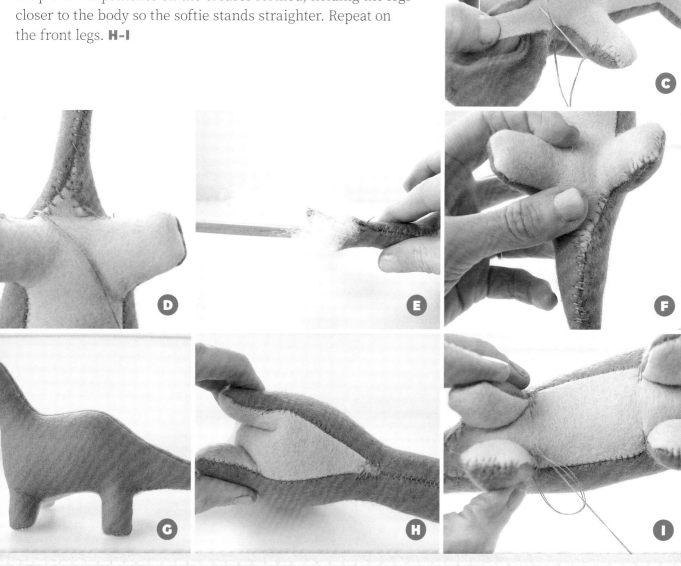

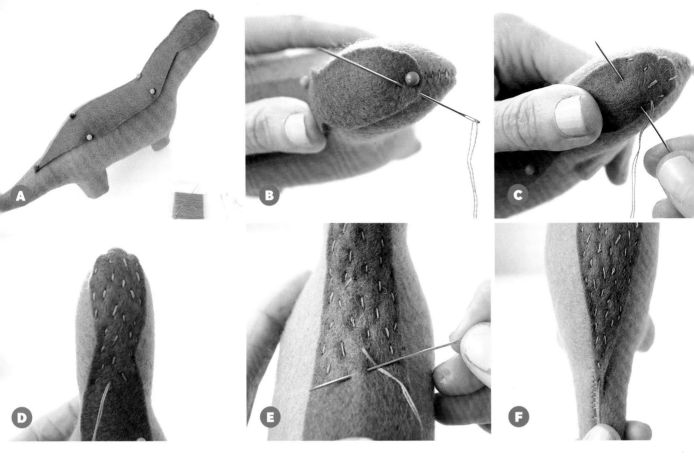

Add the Details

Add the Embroidery

1. Pin piece C to the top of the head, matching the marks on the pattern. **A**

2. Thread the hand-sewing needle with the bright orange embroidery floss. Insert the needle at the top of the head as shown to begin securing piece C to the body. Make a small straight stitch (page 20). Repeat to make a second straight stitch overlapping the edge of piece C. **B**

3. Seed stitch (page 21) down the length of piece C, scattering the small stitches down the neck and back. All the stitches should be vertical, though they might vary slightly in size and angle. **C–F**

4. Sew 3 evenly spaced, vertical straight stitches on each leg. **G-H**

5. At the front of the chest, insert the needle horizontally. Stitch stripes across the peach section with long, evenly spaced straight stitches. **I-L**

Add the Face

1. Draw the eyes with the fabric pen as marked on the pattern. **M**

2. Dip the tip of a pin into the black paint. Slowly and carefully, poke the painted end of the pin into the softie where the eye is marked. Slowly remove it. Repeat on the other eye. Let dry completely before touching to avoid smudging. **N-O**

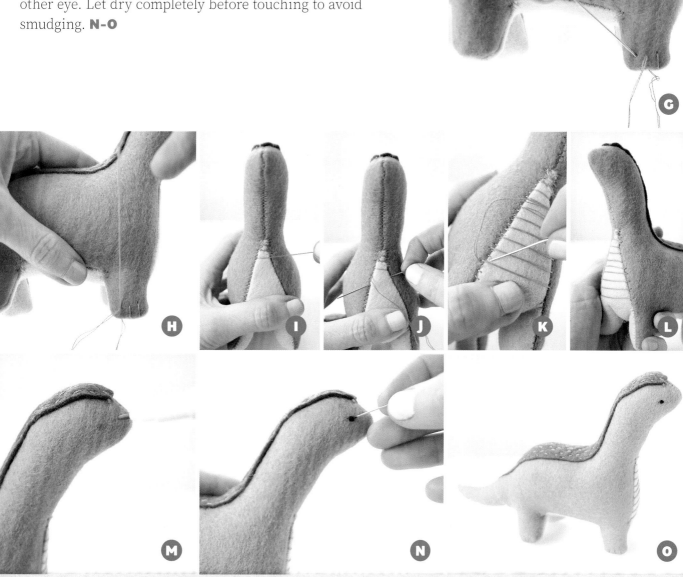

Carnival Giraffe

Cotton candy, popcorn, snow cones, and a dreamy
giraffe painted with all the colors of the carnival.

Materials

8″ × 12″ sheets of merino wool felt in white and pastel yellow

Fine to mid-weight yarn in mint green

Masking or washi tape

Scissors

Fabric pen or pencil

Sewing machine

All-purpose thread in white

Hand-sewing needle

Embroidery floss in bright turquoise

Sewing pins

Polyfill stuffing

Dowel rod (or similar tool)

Acrylic gouache in yellow, light blue, pink, and black

Spray bottle with rubbing alcohol or water

Round paint brushes

Small cups or palette for mixing paint (one per color)

Hand towel or paper towel

Carnival Giraffe templates (pages 130–131)

TEMPLATES

Before beginning the project, print or trace the needed templates onto paper or cardstock. For this project, you need Carnival Giraffe Templates A–E.

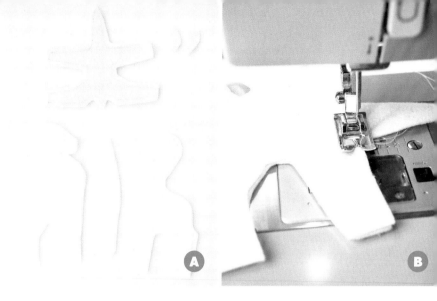

Cut & Sew

1. Trace the templates onto the felt sheet with the fabric pen. Trace 2 of Template E. Trace pieces C and E on the pastel yellow felt and the rest of the pieces on the white felt. Be sure to transfer over all pattern marks. Cut out the felt pieces. **A**

2. Layer pieces A and C, right sides together and matching 2 legs. Sew from the dot at the top of the front leg to the dot at the top of the back leg. **B**

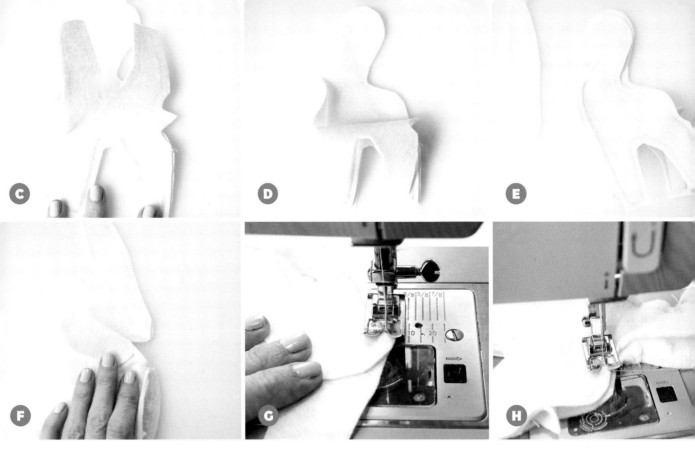

3. Flip over the unit from Step 2. Bend and align the point of piece C with the neck of piece A, matching the *X* marks. Starting with a slight overlap of the stitches in Step 2, sew until you reach the *X*. **C**

4. Fold piece C in half, as shown. Place piece B on top, right sides together and matching up the legs. Sew piece C and piece B together, starting at the top of the back leg and stitching to the *X* mark. **D-E**

5. Lift up the head of piece B. Align the stars on the snout of piece A and the tip of piece D. Bend piece D along piece A and match the triangles. Pin if needed, or bend and align the piece as you sew. Sew from the snout to the triangle mark. Slightly overlap the chest and neck stitches when you start. **F-G**

6. Flip the giraffe over. Align pieces D and B, pinching right sides together. Repeat Step 5 to sew pieces D and B together. When you reach the triangle, continue sewing pieces A and B together for just a few stitches, leaving a gap to stuff the giraffe. **H**

Stuff the Softie

1. Turn the giraffe right side out, poking out all the edges, corners, and points with the dowel rod. **A**

2. Stuff the body with polyfill. Pack it firmly, starting at the tip of the nose and working your way toward the opening until the form is well stuffed. Make sure to press stuffing into each leg. **B**

3. Once the body is well stuffed, begin sewing up the back side. Start by whipstitching (page 13) from the bottom of the gap on one leg to the base of the butt. Tuck in the raw edges. Repeat on the other back leg. Add more stuffing as you stitch to continue to fill out the body. **C-D**

4. Whipstitch the remaining gap closed, again adding more stuffing as you go. Tuck in the raw edges. **E**

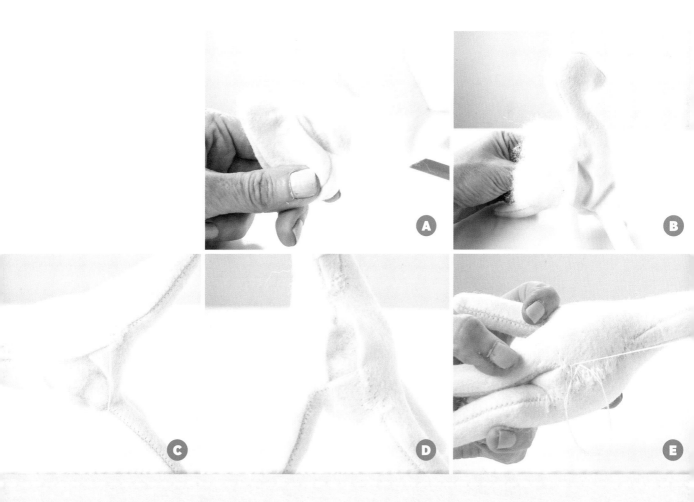

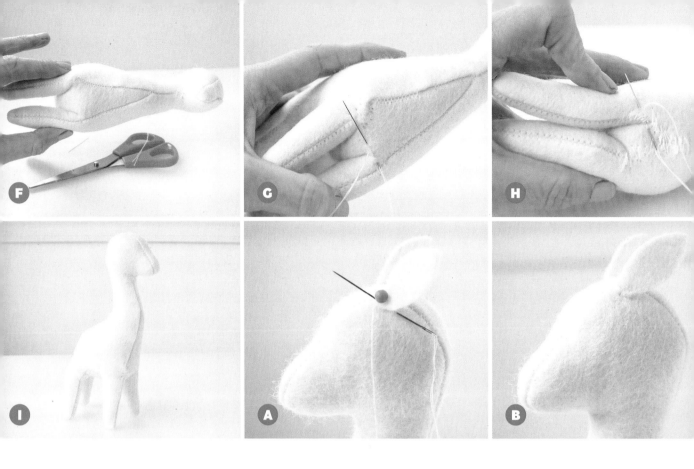

5. Add some additional stitches to improve the structure of the softie. Pinch the front legs together as shown. Add a couple of whipstitches on the creases formed, holding the legs closer to the body so the softie stands straighter. Repeat on the back legs. **F–I**

Add the Details

Attach the Ears

1. Pin both E pieces, the ears, in place. Pin them as marked on the pattern, or adjust them as you prefer. Whipstitch the bottom edge of each ear to the body. **A–B**

Add Color

For this project the desired painted effect is a combination of a pastel wash and defined spots. The paint should be diluted at a ratio of about 1 drop of paint to 20 drops of water. A little dab of paint will go a long way. Once applied, if the color is too light add a small bit more paint to the mixture. For more color mixing tips, see Adding Color (page 15).

1. Mix a wash with each of the 3 colors. Be sure to mix well, taking time to dissolve all the paint with your brush. **C**

2. Mist the giraffe's snout with the spray bottle filled with rubbing alcohol or water. Lightly spray the rest of the body with 1–2 mists. Small droplets will be visible on the material. Spray the nose well, and leave the body mostly dry.

3. Dip the brush into the yellow paint mixture and lightly press it against the snout. Add more yellow dabs to the face, head, and top of the neck. **D-E**

4. Add more defined dots of yellow paint around the body, avoiding the legs. **F-G**

5. Repeat Step 4 to add pink dots to the body. **H**

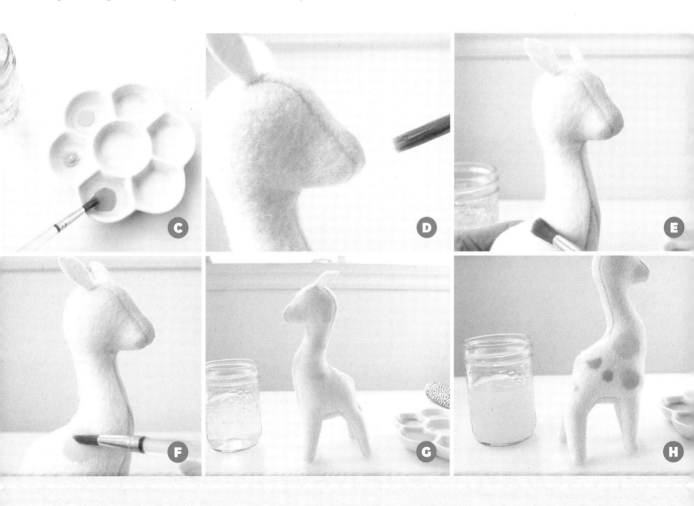

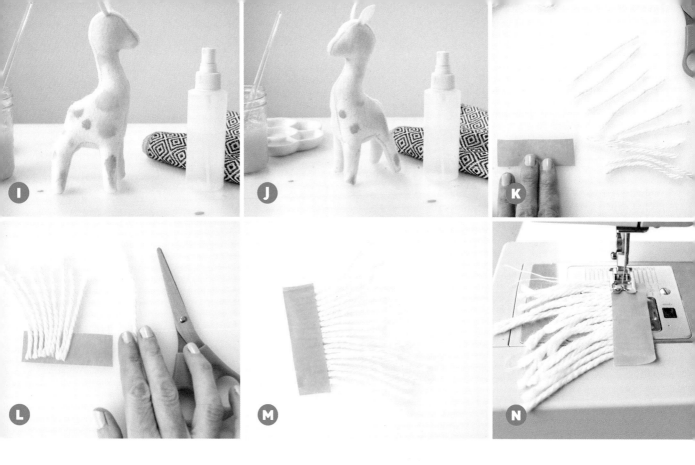

6. Add defined dots of blue paint to the legs. Let the paint dry completely. As the paint dries, it will lighten in color. Add additional layers of paint if you want brighter highlights or washes. **I-J**

Attach the Mane and Tail

1. Cut the green yarn into 3″ pieces. Cut a strip of tape 3″ long and place it sticky side up. **K**

2. Line up the pieces of yarn in a straight line across the tape. The pieces of yarn should touch one another. Fill the whole piece of tape. Cut a second 3″ piece of tape and sandwich the yarn. **L-M**

3. On the sewing machine, stitch through the tape and yarn with a straight line. Repeat with a second line of stitches to secure the mane. Cut away any excess tape or yarn more than ¼″ beyond the seam. **N**

4. Cut 6 pieces of yarn 6″ long and align them for the tail. Use an additional piece of yarn to tie the pieces together. **O**

5. Divide the tail into 3 parts. Braid the tail halfway down, then tie the braid off with a final piece of yarn. **P**

6. Cut a slit in the top of the giraffe's head about 3″ long. Refer to the marks on the pattern. I know it's a bit scary to slice your creation after all the work it took to get here, but I promise it will be worth it! **Q**

7. Slip the tape side of the mane into the slit, sliding it directly under one side of the felt and into the stuffing. Pin it in place. **R-S**

8. Flip the piece upside down, and starting at the bottom of the mane, begin to stitch the gap closed with a whipstitch. **T**

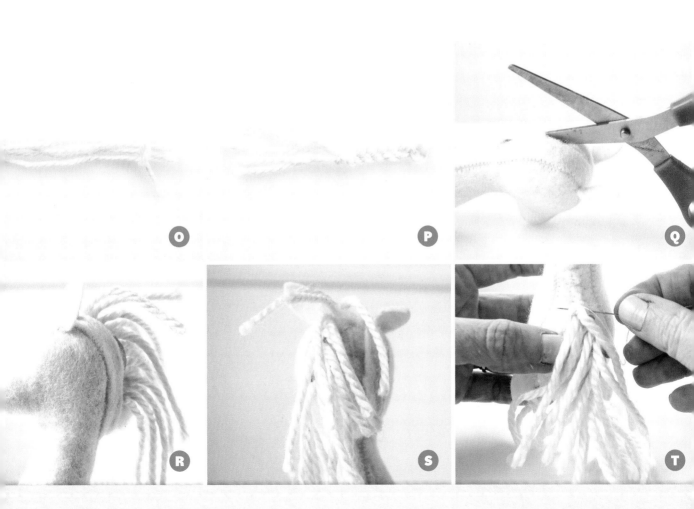

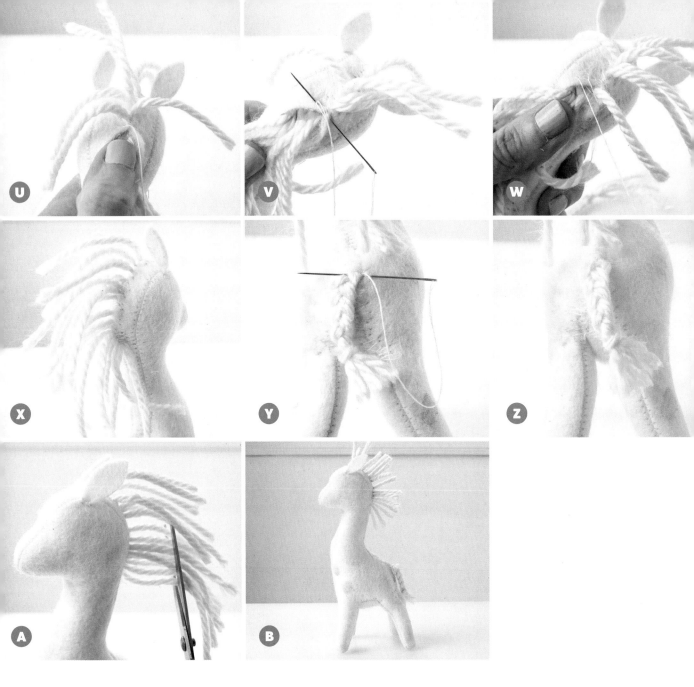

9. Once you reach the yarn, weave the needle between each piece of yarn to join the felt on either side of the mane. If the gap is too big to bridge with 1 stitch, add a second or third. As you pull the gap tight against the mane, the tape should become invisible within the softie. Continue until the gap is closed, and tie off with a knot flush to the softie. **U-X**

10. Trim the bottom of the tail a bit shorter if desired. Pin to the butt. Stitch to the giraffe with a whipstitch. **Y-Z**

11. Time for a haircut! Trim the mane to an even length of about 1″ long. **A-B**

Add the Face

1. Use the fabric marker to mark the eyes from the pattern. **C**

2. Dip the tip of a pin into the black paint. Slowly and carefully, poke the painted end of the pin into the softie where the eye is marked. Slowly remove it. Repeat on the other eye. Let dry completely before touching to avoid smudging.

3. Thread the needle with the bright turquoise floss. Make a small knot at the loose ends of the thread. Cut away any tail on the other side of the knot. **D**

4. Push the needle into the snout and out through the chin to create a nostril, pulling the thread all the way through so the knot is flush. Tie off the thread below the chin. Repeat to create the second nostril. **E–G**

5. Seed stitch (page 21) 3–4 freckles on each cheek. **H–J**

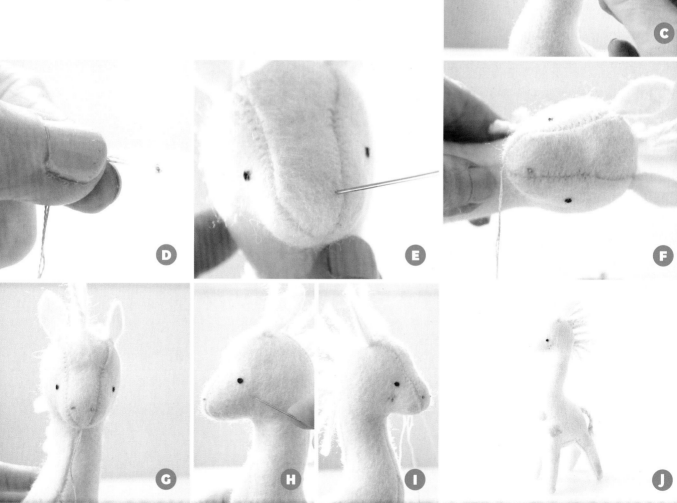

Baby Triceratops

Who says dinosaurs can't be blue? The truth is, no one really knows for sure what color dinosaur scales were back in the prehistoric era. So, I say choose whatever colors you want!

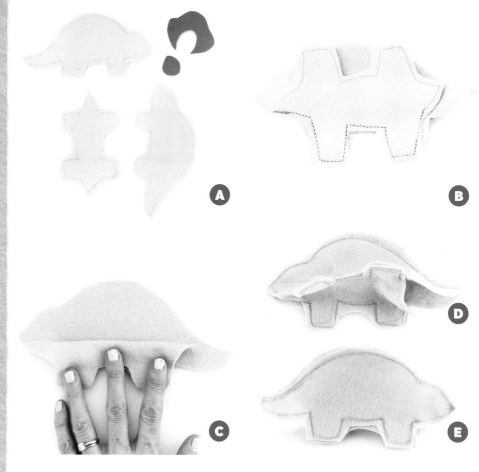

Materials

8″ × 12″ sheets of merino wool felt in light blue and cobalt blue

Scrap of white felt about 4″ × 4″

Scissors

Fabric pen or pencil

Sewing machine

All-purpose sewing thread in turquoise and white

Hand-sewing needle

Embroidery floss in bright turquoise

Sewing pins

Polyfill stuffing

Dowel rod (or similar tool)

Acrylic gouache in black

Baby Triceratops templates (pages 132–133)

TEMPLATES

Before beginning your project, print or trace the needed templates onto paper or cardstock. For this project, you need Baby Triceratops Templates A–G.

Cut & Sew

1. Trace Templates A, B, and C onto the light blue felt sheet with the fabric pen. Trace Templates D and E onto the cobalt blue felt sheet. Be sure to transfer over all pattern marks. Save templates F and G and the white felt for later. Cut out the felt pieces. **A**

2. Align piece C with piece A, right sides together, and with one set of the feet matched up. Align the dot of piece C with the dot of piece A. Sew from the triangle at the tip of the nose to the dot at the top of the back leg. **B**

3. Fold piece C in half, bringing the other set of feet down. Place piece B on top, right sides together, and matching up the feet and the Xs. Repeat Step 2 to sew together. Do not sew through piece A during this stage. **C**

4. Sew pieces A and B together, starting by overlapping the existing stitches at the nose, and continuing over the triceratops's back to the tip of the tail. **D-E**

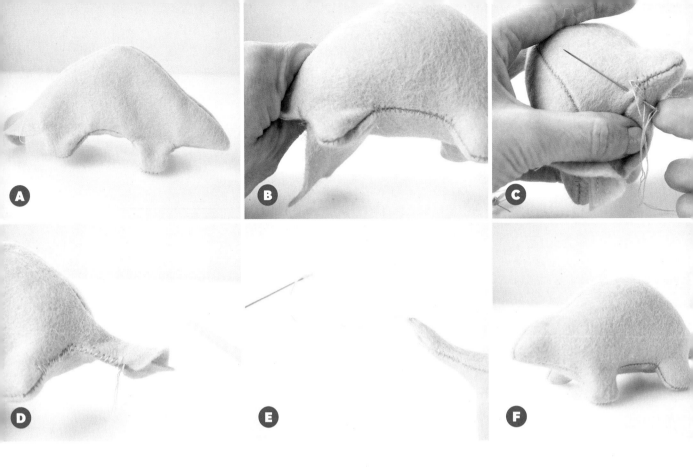

Stuff the Softie

1. Turn the dinosaur right side out, poking out all the edges, corners, and points with the dowel rod. **A**

2. Stuff the body with polyfill. Pack it firmly, starting at the tip of the nose and working your way toward the opening until the form is well stuffed. Make sure to press stuffing into each leg. **B**

3. Hand sew the opening at the back of the tail with a whipstitch (page 13) and turquoise thread, tucking in the raw edges. Start at one leg and continue to the base of the tail. Add stuffing as you sew to fill out the form completely. Repeat on the other leg. Then, begin to stitch up the sides of the tail. Add more stuffing as you go to fill it out. Finally, whipstitch the bottom side of the tail to the point, creating a round shape. **C-F**

4. Add some additional stitches to improve the structure of the softie. Pinch the back legs together as shown. Add a couple of whipstitches on the creases formed, holding the legs closer to the body so the softie stands straighter. Repeat on the front legs. **G-H**

Add the Details

1. Pin piece E around the neck as shown. Pin piece D on top of the head, making sure the edges slightly overlap piece E. **A-B**

2. Starting at one side of piece E, use the bright turquoise embroidery floss to whipstitch it to the softie and piece D around the whole inner curve. **C-E**

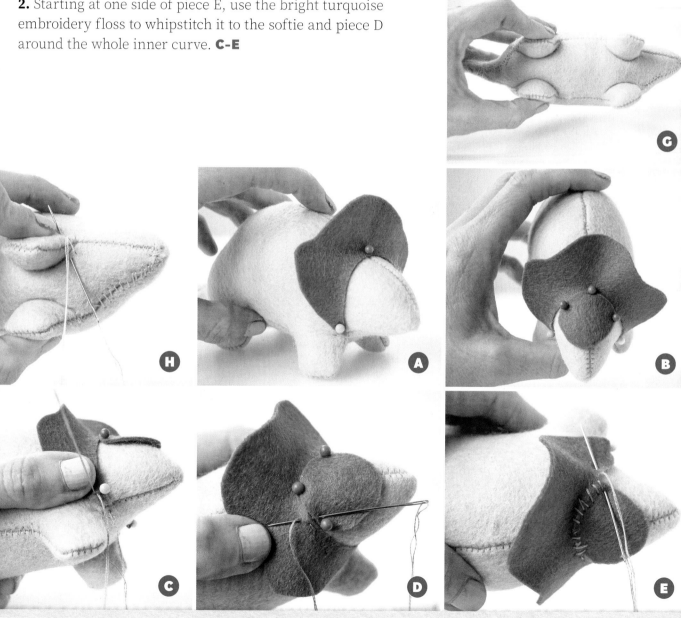

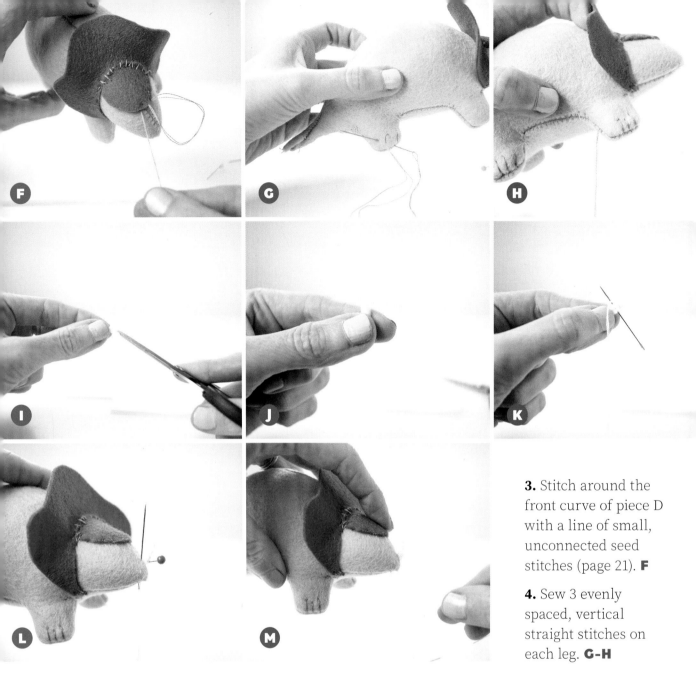

3. Stitch around the front curve of piece D with a line of small, unconnected seed stitches (page 21). **F**

4. Sew 3 evenly spaced, vertical straight stitches on each leg. **G-H**

Add the Horns

1. Cut Template G (or freehand cut a small triangle about ½″ long) from the white felt scrap. This will be the small horn for the tip of the nose. **I**

2. Roll the felt between your fingers to create a rounded cone shape. With the white thread, whipstitch the open side of the horn from the top to the bottom to hold the shape. **J-K**

3. Pin the horn to the tip of the nose. Whipstitch the horn to the softie with the white thread. **L-M**

4. Trace Template F onto the remaining white felt twice and cut out. Repeat Steps 2–3 to roll both triangles into crescent shape pointed horns and secure them with whipstitches. **N**

5. Pin the horns to the head at the edges of piece D. Whipstitch the horns to the softie with the white thread. **O-Q**

Add the Eyes

1. Draw the eyes with the fabric pen as marked on the pattern. **R**

2. Dip the tip of a pin into the black paint. Slowly and carefully, poke the painted end of the pin into the softie where the eye is marked. Slowly remove it. Repeat on the other eye. Let dry completely before touching to avoid smudging. **S-U**

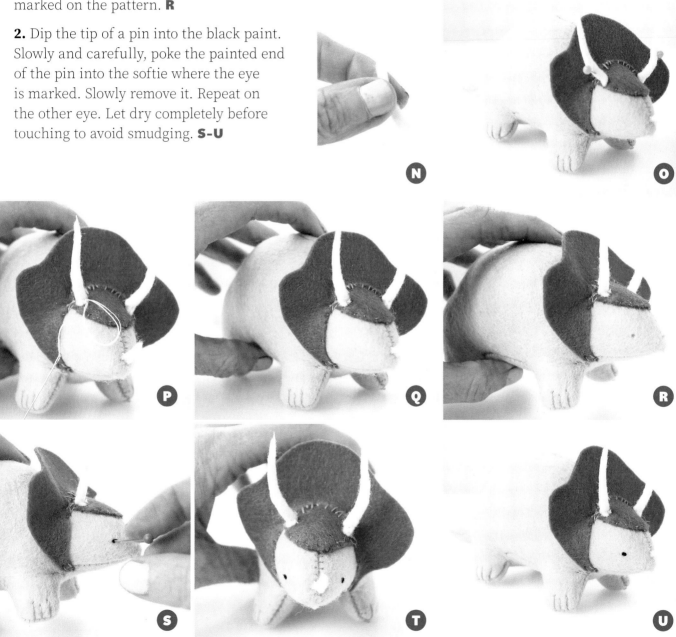

Fluffy Lion

This sweet pink lion with an untamed mane is the king of cute! Make a whole pride in a rainbow of pastels.

Materials

8″ × 12″ sheet of merino wool felt in baby pink

1″ × 5½″ strip of baby pink long pile mongolian fur

Fabric pen or pencil

Scissors

Sewing machine

Matching all-purpose sewing thread

Hand-sewing needle

Embroidery floss in black

Sewing pins

Polyfill stuffing

Dowel rod (or similar tool)

Acrylic gouache in black

Fluffy Lion templates (pages 133–134)

TEMPLATES

Before beginning the project, print or trace the needed templates onto paper or cardstock. For this project, you need Fluffy Lion Templates A–G.

Cut & Sew

1. Trace the templates onto the felt sheet with the fabric pen. Trace 2 of Template E. Be sure to transfer over all pattern marks. Cut out the felt pieces. **A**

2. Trace Template G onto the faux fur. Cut out and set aside.

3. Layer pieces A and D right sides together, matching the point of piece D with the snout on piece A. Sew together along the short flat edge. **B**

4. Pull down the long top edge of piece D, aligning it with the top edge of piece A. The end of piece D should align with the star mark at the center back. Pin if needed. Sew together, starting at the mark and stitching toward the snout. **C**

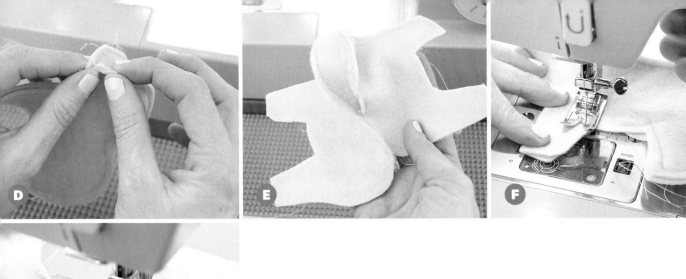

5. Lift up the flap of piece D and align it with the snout and top edge of piece B, right sides together. The point of D and the snout points on pieces A and B should all meet. Pin if needed, keeping piece A out of the way. Starting from the tip of the snout, sew piece B to piece D until you reach the end of piece D. Then, align pieces A and B, and continue sewing A and B together to the triangle mark. **D-E**

6. Pull pieces A and B apart, then sandwich piece C between them, aligning all 4 legs right sides together. Sew piece A to piece C from the dot mark at the top of the back leg to the snout point, overlapping the existing stitching slightly. At the chest, align one edge of the piece C tip with piece A and continue sewing. Do not sew through piece B when attaching pieces A and C.

Repeat on the other side, attaching pieces B and C from the top of the back leg to the chin. Do not sew through piece A when attaching pieces B and C. **F-G**

Stuff the Softie

1. Turn the lion right side out, poking out all the edges, corners, and points with the dowel rod. **A**

2. Stuff the body with polyfill. Pack it firmly, starting at the tip of the nose and working your way toward the opening until the form is well stuffed. Make sure to press stuffing into each leg. **B**

3. Hand sew the opening at the back of the tail with a whipstitch (page 13), tucking in the raw edges. Start at one leg and continue to the base of the body. Add stuffing as you sew to fill out the form completely. Repeat on the other leg. You want the lion to be round and plush. Once the legs are closed stitched together, whipstitch the remaining gap closed. **C-E**

4. Add some additional stitches to improve the structure of the softie. Pinch the back legs together as shown. Add a couple of whipstitches on the creases formed, holding the legs closer to the body so the softie stands straighter. Repeat on the front legs. **F-G**

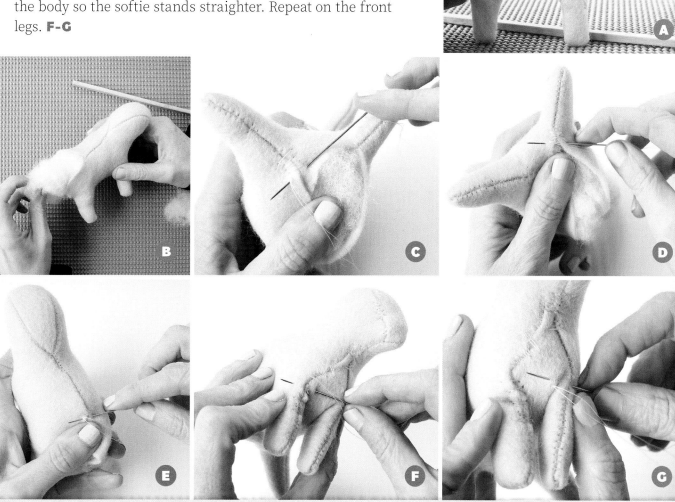

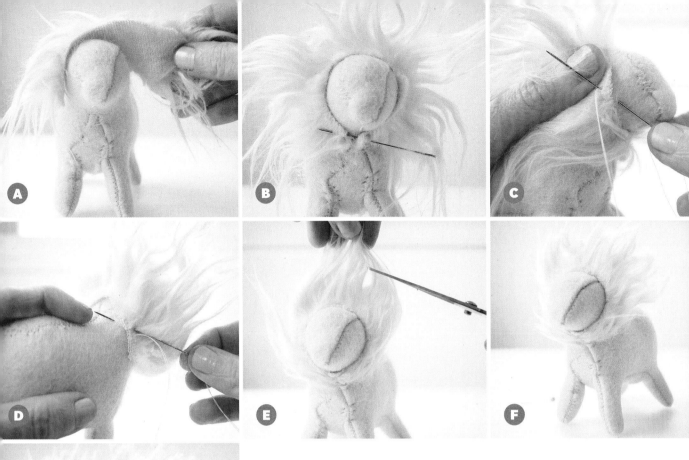

Add the Details

Attach the Mane

1. Drape the piece G piece of fur over the lion's head. Pin the ends under the lion's chin. **A-B**

2. Whipstitch around the inner curve of the mane, securing the fur to the softie all the way around the head. Repeat on the outer curve of the strip around the head. **C-D**

3. Fluff the mane so it stands up. Then, trim the mane all the way around, leaving about 1″ of fur. **E-F**

Attach the Ears and Tail

1. Pin both E pieces, the ears, in place as marked on the pattern, or adjust them as you prefer. Whipstitch the ears to the head. **G**

2. To make the tail, roll piece F back and forth between your fingers, creating a rounded shape. Tuck a scrap of faux fur into the bottom of the felt piece. Whipstitch the tail into shape, securing the fur, along the open side. Stitch halfway up the length of the tail. **H-J**

3. Pin the tail in place as marked on the pattern, or as you prefer. Whipstitch the tail to the body. **K**

Add the Face

1. With the fabric marker, draw the eyes, nose, and mouth as marked on the pattern. **L**

2. Begin embroidering the lion's nose. Stitch overlapping horizontal straight stitches (page 20). Stitch a small triangle. At the base of the nose, stitch 2 diagonal straight stitches for the mouth. **M-N**

3. Dip the tip of a pin into the black paint. Slowly and carefully, poke the painted end of the pin into the softie where the eye is marked. Slowly remove it. Repeat on the other eye. Let dry completely before touching to avoid smudging. **O-Q**

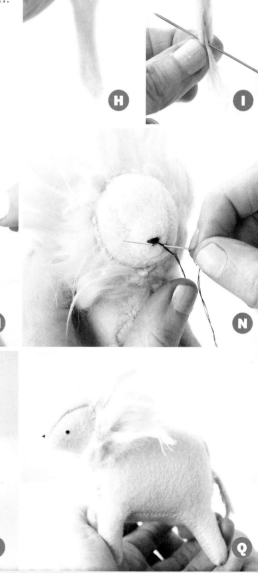

Folktale Wolf

The folktale wolf is the perfect companion on a chilly, northern night. Her magical eyes tell woodland stories and forest secrets to any who lean in and listen.

Materials

8″ × 12″ sheets of merino wool felt in heather gray and mint green

Scissors

Fabric pen or pencil

Sewing machine

All-purpose sewing thread in gray

Hand-sewing needle

Embroidery floss in, orange, yellow, and black

Sewing pins

Polyfill stuffing

Dowel rod (or similar tool)

Folktale Wolf templates (pages 135–136)

TEMPLATES

Before beginning your project, print or trace the needed templates onto paper or cardstock. For this project, you need Folktale Wolf Templates A–F.

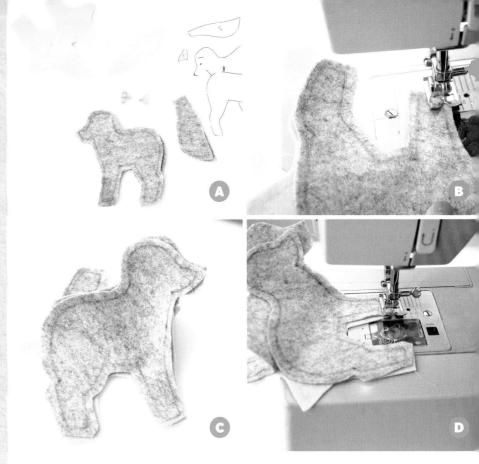

Cut & Sew

1. Trace the templates onto the felt sheet with the fabric pen. Trace Templates A, B, E, and F on the gray felt. Trace Templates C and D on the mint green felt. Trace 2 of piece E. Be sure to transfer over all pattern marks. Cut out the felt pieces. **A**

2. Layer piece B over piece C, right sides together and matching dots and Xs. The tip of piece C should line up with the neck and chest of piece B. Pin if needed. Starting at the mark at the top of the back leg, sew all the way to the star on the chest and the tip of piece C. **B**

3. Flip over the unit from Step 2. Fold piece C in half toward the bottom of the wolf, then layer piece A on top (right sides together), lining up the legs and chest. Sew piece A and piece C together, starting at the star on the chest and sewing to the mark at the top of the back leg. **C-D**

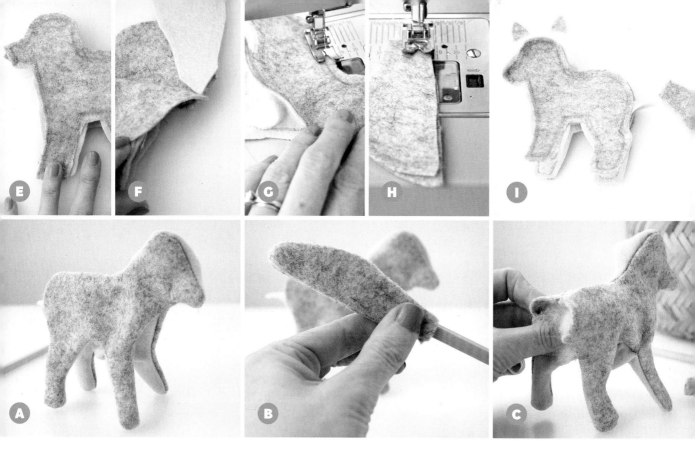

4. Sew pieces A and B together from the star on the chest to the triangle at the snout. Slightly overlap the stitching from Step 3 to start. **E**

5. Align the triangle mark on the point of piece D with the snout on piece B, right sides together. Starting by slightly overlapping the stitching from Step 4, stitch the 2 pieces together to the double triangle at the back of the neck. **F**

6. Repeat Step 5 to sew piece D to piece A. Pinch piece D in half so they are aligned right sides together. When you reach the end of piece D, continue stitching pieces A and B together until the star above the butt. **G**

7. Layer the F pieces right sides together. Sew around the exterior of the shape, leaving a gap along the short, flat edge. **H-I**

Stuff the Softie

1. Turn the wolf right side out, poking out all the edges, corners, and points with the dowel rod. Turn the tail (F pieces) right side out. **A-B**

2. Stuff the body with polyfill. Pack it firmly, starting at the tip of the nose and working your way toward the opening until the form is well stuffed. Make sure to press stuffing into each leg. **C**

3. Begin sewing up the back side. Start by whipstitching (page 13) from the bottom of the gap on one leg to the top of the leg triangle. Tuck in the raw edges. Repeat on the other back leg, completely closing the gap. Add more stuffing as you stitch to continue to fill out the body. **D-F**

4. Add some additional stitches to improve the structure of the softie. Pinch the back legs together as shown. Add a couple of whipstitches on the creases formed, holding the legs closer to the body so the softie stands straighter. Repeat on the front legs. **G-I**

5. Stuff the tail with polyfill. **J**

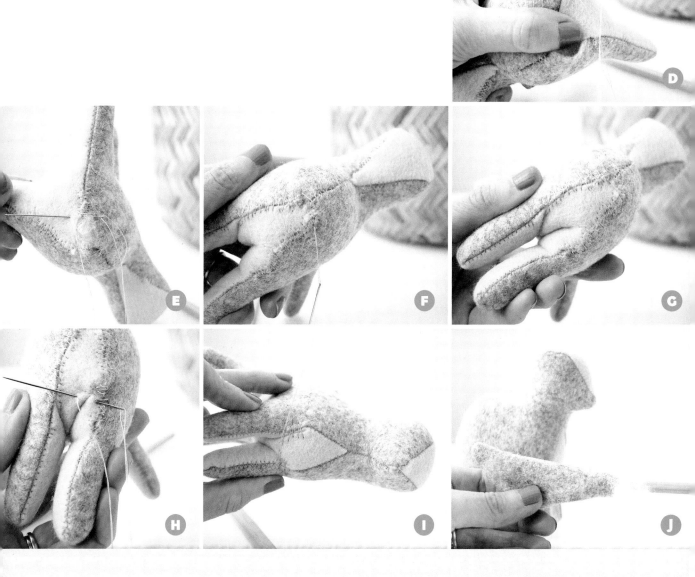

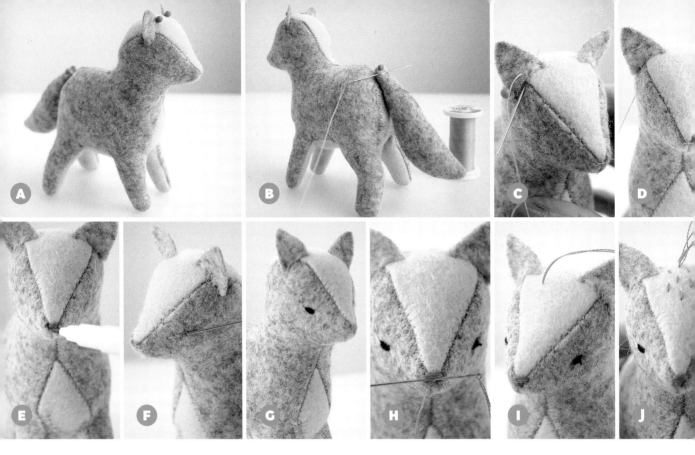

Add the Details

Attach the Ears and Tail

1. Pin both D pieces, the ears, in place as marked on the pattern, or as you desire. Repeat with the tail, pinning at the top of the butt. **A**

2. Whipstitch the tail and ears to the softie with the gray thread. **B-D**

Add the Face and Embroidery

1. Use the fabric marker to mark the eyes and the nose from the pattern. Thread the needle with black floss. **E**

2. Stitch an almond shape for each eye using short straight stitches (page 20). **F-G**

3. Using the orange floss, insert the needle at the top of the marked nose, going out the other side. Pull the needle through. Repeat the process, stitching small, horizontal straight stitches that are progressively shorter and overlap with one another to create a triangle shape for the nose. Make a knot at the bottom of the nose, then insert the needle so it comes out at the top of the head. **H-I**

4. Seed stitch (page 21) 6–8 vertical stitches on the wolf's forehead. **J**

5. Rethread the needle with the orange thread. Cut the tail away from the knot. **K**

6. Insert the needle directly through the center of one eye, pulling the knot flush against the softie. Repeat on the other eye. Remember to exit through a seam so you can hide the thread tail inside the softie. **L-M**

7. Draw the thistle design with the fabric pen as marked on the template. Stitch the thistle (see Embroidery Motif Library, page 22) on the neck of the wolf with straight stitches. Add several overlapping straight stitches for the bud. Use black, yellow, and orange floss. Repeat on the other side of the body. **N-T**

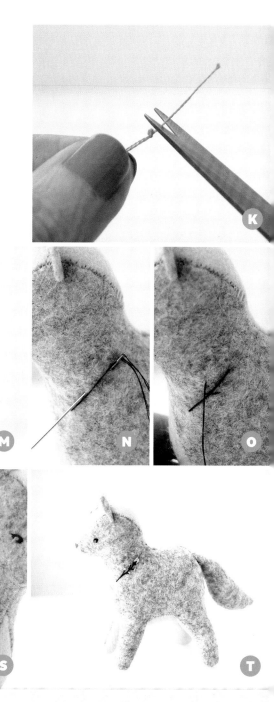

Rainbow Reef Orca

This enchanting prismatic orca is a magical creature of the deep. The soft black felt and intricate stitching mimics the vibrant hues of underwater coral reefs.

Cut & Sew

1. Trace the templates onto the felt sheets with the fabric pen. Trace Templates A, B, and D onto black felt. Trace Templates C, E, and F onto white felt. Trace 2 each of Templates D, E, and F. Be sure to transfer over all pattern marks. Cut out the felt pieces. **A**

2. Align pieces A and B, wrong sides together. Pin if desired. Hand sew with a whipstitch (page 13), tucking in the raw edges as you sew. Stitch from the tip of the nose, over the back and fin, and to the dot on the tail. Gently pull the stitches taut; you want them flush with the felt, but not causing puckering or indents. **B-C**

3. Layer the unit from Step 2 over piece C, matching pattern marks. Pin if desired. Starting at the tip of the nose, whipstitch piece C to the unit from Step 2. Stop when you reach the first fin, tie a knot and trim the thread, then pick up the stitching on the other side of the fin, leaving a gap. Stitch to the base of the tail, and leave a gap at the tail fins. Continue up the other side. **D-E**

4. Align piece D (the fin) with the fin on piece A. Whipstitch the connection point between piece D and piece C, closing the gap but leaving the fin flaps open. Repeat on the other side. Leave the tail open for stuffing. **F-G**

Stuff the Softie

1. Stuff the body with polyfill. Pack it firmly, starting at the tip of the nose and working your way toward the opening at the tail until the form is well stuffed. **A**

2. Sew the back tail fin closed with a whipstitch, beginning at the center of the tail and moving around the first half of the fin. Repeat on the other side of the tail. **B-C**

Add the Details

Attach the Patches

1. Pin the 2 eye (E) and 2 tail (F) patches where indicated on the pattern. **A**

2. With white thread, whipstitch the exterior of the patches to the softie. **B**

Add the Embroidery

1. Draw the embroidered designs with the fabric pen as marked on the template. On one side of the orca, draw a spiral coral, 2 fringed branches, and a star coral. On the other side, draw a sweeping branch, 2 star coral, and an anemone coral. **C-D**

2. Stitch the designs (see Embroidery Motif Library, page 22). Stitch the spiral coral with a yellow chain stitch (page 21). Stitch 1 fringed branch with an orange straight stitch (page 20) and the other with a red straight stitch. Stitch the star coral with a cream straight stitch. Add a couple of cream seed stitches (page 21) nearby. **E**

3. On the other side, stitch the sweeping branch with a turquoise chain stitch. Stitch the anemone with a red straight stitch. Stitch 1 star coral in orange and the other in cream. Add a couple of seed stitches in cream. **F**

4. Whipstitch the outside perimeter of the fins closed. **G-H**

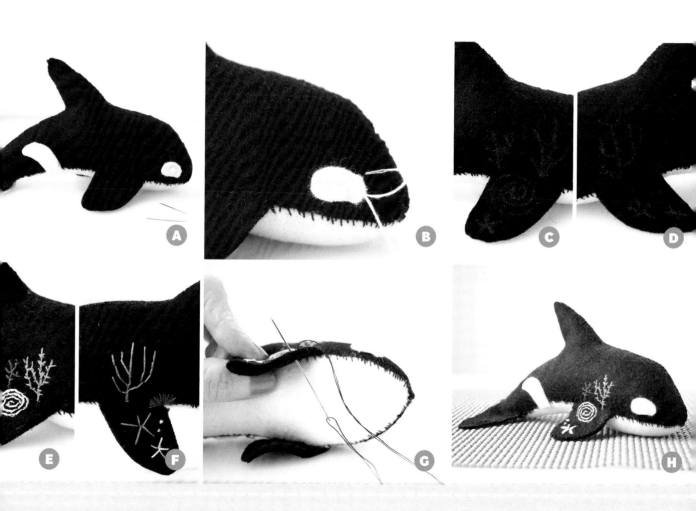

Baby Hippo

Here comes trouble. Hippos are the biggest babies on the riverbank, and this one's here to steal your heart (and your snacks)!

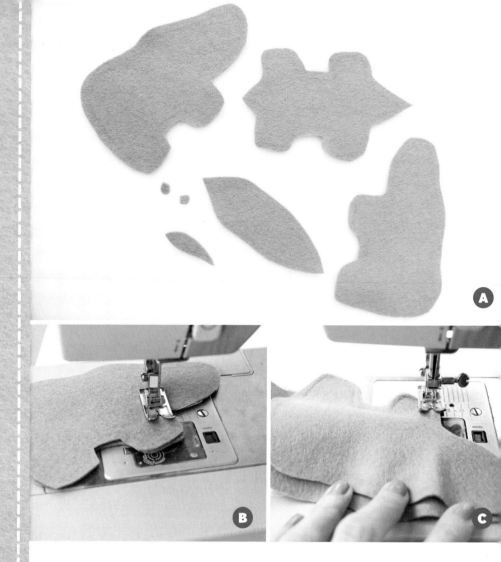

Materials

8″ × 12″ sheet of merino wool felt in fuchsia

Scissors

Fabric pen or pencil

Sewing machine

Matching all-purpose sewing thread

Hand-sewing needle

Embroidery floss in pink

Sewing pins

Polyfill stuffing

Dowel rod (or similar tool)

Acrylic gouache in black

Baby Hippo templates (pages 139–140)

TEMPLATES

Before beginning your project, print or trace the needed templates onto paper or cardstock. For this project, you need Baby Hippo Templates A–F.

Cut & Sew

1. Trace the templates onto the felt sheet with the fabric pen. Trace 2 of Template E. Be sure to transfer over all pattern marks. Cut out the felt pieces. **A**

2. Align pieces A and C, right sides together and matching marks. The tip of piece C should line up with the tip at the neck and chest of piece A. Pin if needed. Starting at the tip of piece C at the chin, sew to the dot at the top of the back leg. **B**

3. Flip over the unit from Step 2. Fold piece C in half toward the bottom of the hippo, then layer piece B on top (right sides together), lining up the legs and chin. Sew piece B and piece C together, starting at the X at the top of the back leg and sewing to the triangle at the chin. **C**

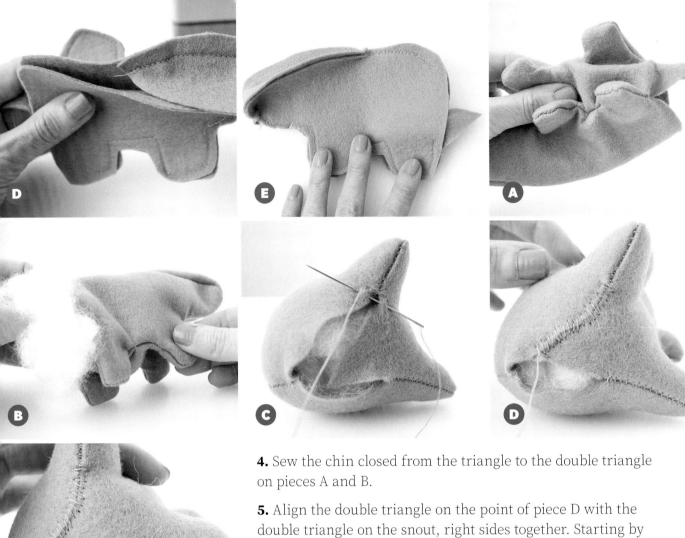

4. Sew the chin closed from the triangle to the double triangle on pieces A and B.

5. Align the double triangle on the point of piece D with the double triangle on the snout, right sides together. Starting by slightly overlapping the stitching from Step 4, stitch the two pieces together to the mark at the back of the neck. **D**

6. Repeat Step 5 to sew piece D to piece A. Pinch piece D in half so the pieces are aligned right sides together. When you reach the end of piece D, continue stitching pieces A and B together until the tail mark above the butt. **E**

Stuff the Softie

1. Turn the hippo right side out, poking out all the edges, corners, and points with the dowel rod. **A**

2. Stuff the body with polyfill. Pack it firmly, starting at the tip of the nose and working your way toward the opening until the form is well stuffed. Make sure to press stuffing into each leg. **B**

3. Begin sewing up the back side. Start by whipstitching (page 13) from the bottom of the gap on one leg to the top of the leg triangle. Tuck in the raw edges. Repeat on the other back leg. Add more stuffing as you stitch to continue to fill out the body. **C-E**

4. Add a small amount of stuffing, then close the remaining gap. **F**

5. Add some additional stitches to improve the structure of the softie. Pinch the back legs together as shown. Add a couple of whipstitches on the creases formed, holding the legs closer to the body so the softie stands straighter. Repeat on the front legs. **G-H**

Add the Details

Attach the Ears and Tail

1. Pin both E pieces, the ears, in place. Pin them as marked on pieces A and B, or adjust them as you prefer. **A**

2. To make the tail, roll piece F back and forth between your fingers, creating a rounded shape. Whipstitch the tail into shape with the matching thread along the open side. Stitch most of the length of the tail, leaving the ends open. Pin the tail in place on the back seam above the butt. **B-D**

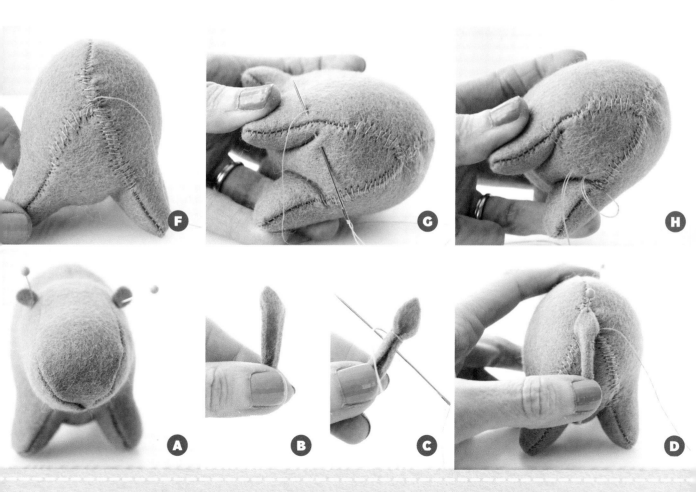

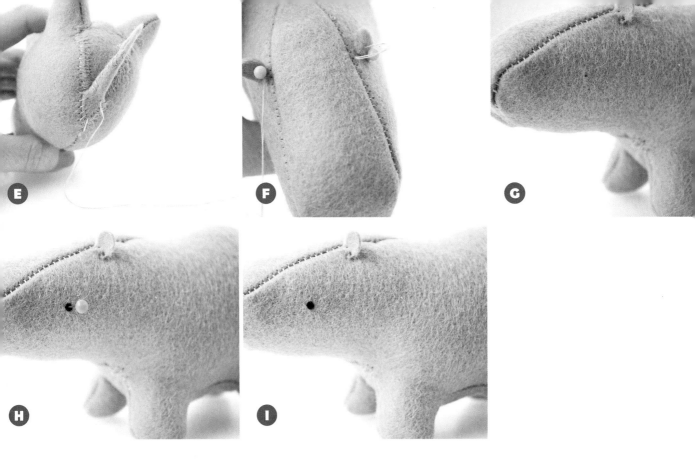

3. Whipstitch the tail and ears to the softie. **E-F**

Add the Eyes

1. With the fabric marker, draw the eyes as marked on the pattern or as you prefer. **G**

Tip
If the marks from your fabric pen are ever too hard to see on the softie, use pins to mark the facial expressions instead. It can be good to keep a couple different marking tools around for use on different colors of felt.

2. Dip the tip of a pin into the black paint. Slowly and carefully, poke the painted end of the pin into the softie where the eye is marked. Slowly remove it. Repeat on the other eye. Let dry completely before touching to avoid smudging. **H-I**

Add the Embroidery

1. Thread the needle with the pink floss. Cut away any thread tail past the knot. Insert the needle into the seam on one side of the snout and pull the knot flush with the softie. The needle should exit opposite the first knot through the other seam. **J-K**

2. Tie a knot with the tail of the thread to make the other nostril. Pull the knot flush with the softie. **L-M**

3. Seed stitch (page 21) a few freckles under each eye with the pink floss. Repeat on the top of the head. **N-Q**

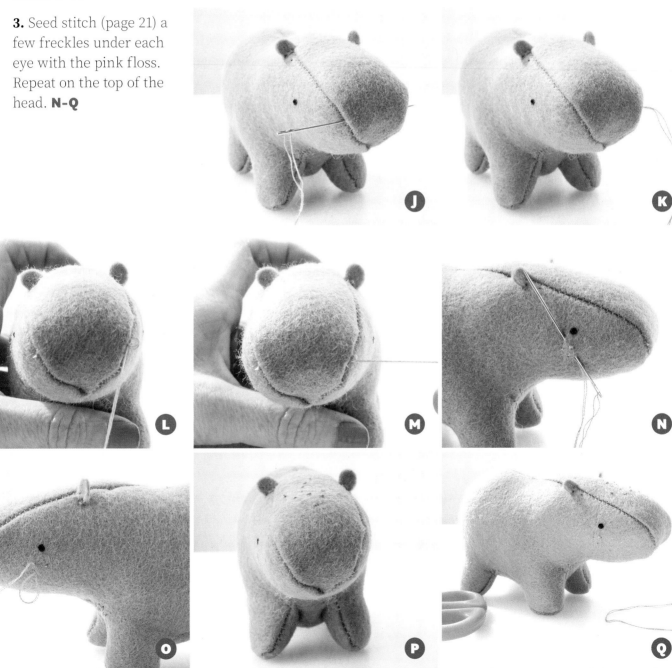

Little Walrus

A cuddly young walrus to lounge on your desk, all round and warm. Tiny tusks, big personality!

Materials

8″ × 12″ sheet of merino wool felt in tan

Scrap of white felt about 3″ × 3″

Scissors

Fabric pen or pencil

Sewing machine

All-purpose sewing thread in tan and white

Hand-sewing needle

Embroidery floss in mustard and rust

Sewing pins

Polyfill stuffing

Dowel rod (or similar tool)

Acrylic gouache in black

Little Walrus templates (pages 140–141)

TEMPLATES

Before beginning your project, print or trace the needed templates onto paper or cardstock. For this project, you need Little Walrus Templates A, B, and C.

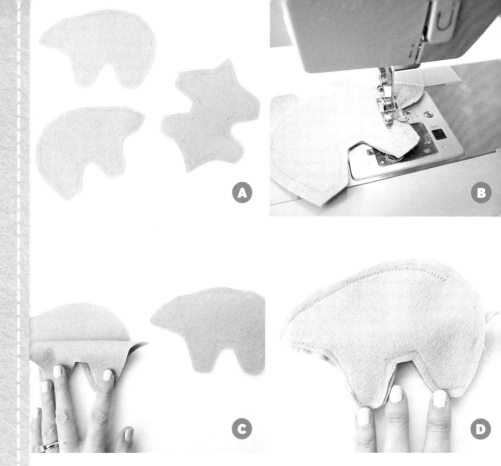

Cut & Sew

1. Trace the templates onto the felt sheet with the fabric pen. Be sure to transfer over all pattern marks. Cut out the felt pieces. **A**

2. Layer piece A over piece C, right sides together and matching dots and Xs. The tip of piece C should line up with the neck and chest of piece A. Pin if needed. Starting at the tip of piece C on the chest, sew all the way to the mark at the top of the back flipper. **B**

3. Flip over the unit from Step 2. Fold piece C in half toward the bottom of the walrus, then layer piece B on top (right sides together), lining up the flippers and chest. Sew piece B and piece C together, starting at the mark at the top of the back flipper and sewing to the chest. **C**

4. Sew pieces A and B together, starting at the triangle mark above the butt and stitching until you overlap the stitching from Steps 2 and 3. **D**

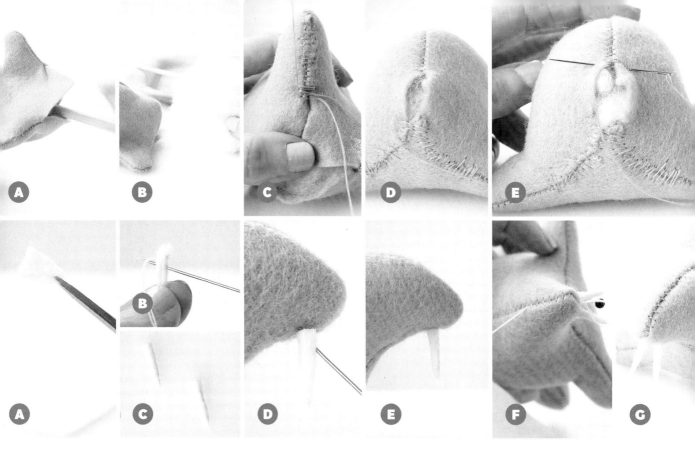

Stuff the Softie

1. Turn the walrus right side out, poking out all the edges, corners, and points with the dowel rod. **A**

2. Stuff the body with polyfill. Pack it firmly, starting at the tip of the nose and working your way toward the opening until the form is well stuffed. Make sure to press stuffing into each flipper. **B**

3. Begin sewing up the back side. Start by whipstitching (page 13) from the bottom of the gap on one flipper to the top of the piece C tip. Tuck in the raw edges. Repeat on the other back flipper. Add more stuffing as you stitch to continue to fill out the body. **C-D**

4. Add a small amount of stuffing, then close the remaining gap. **E**

Add the Details

Attach the Tusks

1. Cut a pair of small triangles about ⅜″ long from the white felt scrap. **A**

2. Roll the felt between your fingers to create a rounded cone shape. With the white thread, whipstitch the open side of the tusk from the top to the bottom to hold the shape. **B-C**

3. Pin the tusks in place under the nose as marked on the pattern. **D**

4. Thread the hand-sewing needle with white thread. Bring the needle down through the top seam and through one tusk. Then, insert the needle back through the tusk and out through the team at the top of the head. Repeat 2–3 times on each tusk. **E-G**

Add the Embroidery

1. Sew 4–5 evenly spaced, vertical straight stitches (page 20) on each flipper with the mustard floss. **H-J**

2. Stitch 3–4 horizontal straight stitches along the walrus's back with the mustard floss. Vary the length of the stripes. Leave space between them. Pull the embroidery floss taut to make the walrus a little lumpy. **K**

3. Repeat Step 2 with the rust floss. Then, add 1 horizontal stitch stitch for the walrus's nose. **L**

Add the Eyes

1. Draw the eyes with the fabric pen as marked on the pattern. **M**

2. Dip the tip of a pin into the black paint. Slowly and carefully, poke the painted end of the pin into the softie where the eye is marked. Slowly remove it. Repeat on the other eye. Let dry completely before touching to avoid smudging. **N-O**

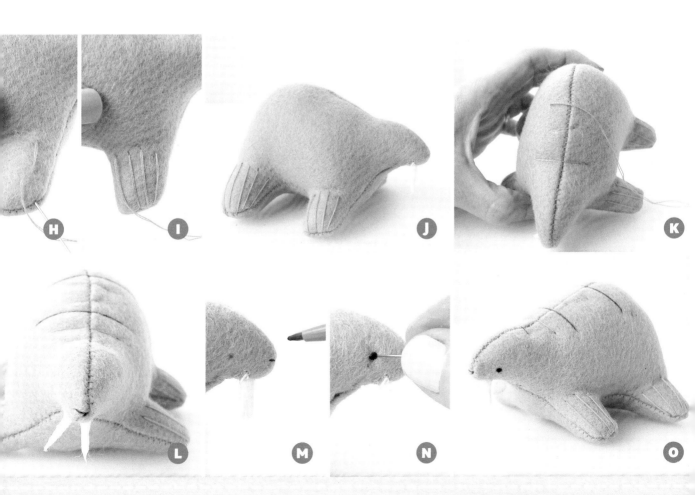

Baby Stegosaurus

This is the cuddliest little herbivore with a heart of gold and tickling spikes. This cutie is my favorite prehistoric friend!

Materials

8″ × 12″ sheets of merino wool felt orange and fuchsia

Scissors

Fabric pen or pencil

Sewing machine

All-purpose sewing thread in orange

Hand-sewing needle

Embroidery floss in mint green

Sewing pins

Polyfill stuffing

Dowel rod (or similar tool)

Acrylic gouache in black

Baby Stegosaurus templates (pages 141–142)

Super glue (optional)

TEMPLATES

Before beginning your project, print or trace the needed templates onto paper or cardstock. For this project, you need Baby Stegosaurus Templates A–D.

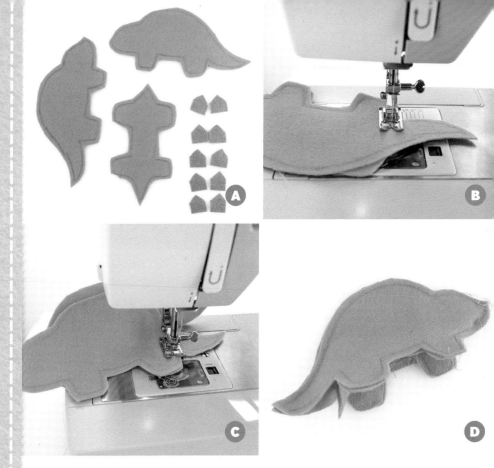

Cut & Sew

1. Trace the templates onto the felt sheet with the fabric pencil. Trace 10 of Template D on the fuchsia felt (mirror half the shapes). Trace Templates A, B, and C on the orange felt. Be sure to transfer over all pattern marks. Cut out the felt pieces. **A**

2. Layer piece A over piece C, right sides together, and with the one set of the feet matched up. Align the tip of piece C with the neck of piece A. Sew from the tip of piece C to the dot at the top of the back leg. **B**

3. Fold piece C in half, bringing the other set of feet down. Place piece B on top, right sides together and matching up the feet. Repeat Step 2 to sew together, this time starting at the back leg. Do not sew through piece A during this stage. **C**

4. Sew pieces A and B together from the tip of the tail until you slightly overlap the stitching from Steps 2 and 3. **D**

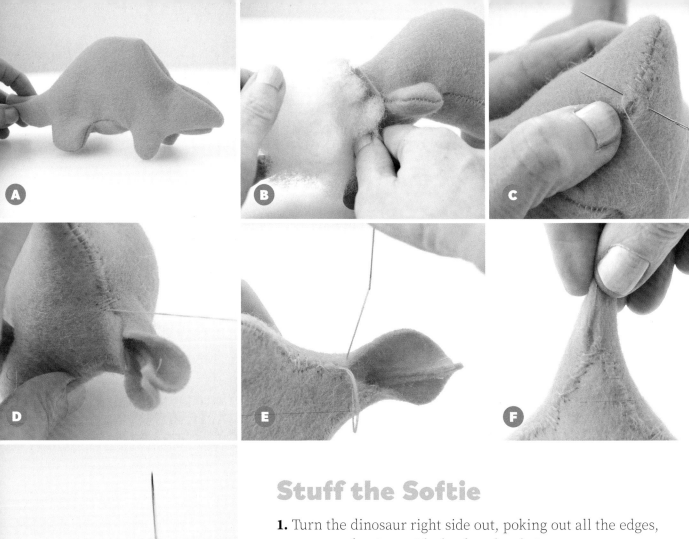

Stuff the Softie

1. Turn the dinosaur right side out, poking out all the edges, corners, and points with the dowel rod. **A**

2. Stuff the body with polyfill. Pack it firmly, starting at the tip of the nose and working your way toward the opening until the form is well stuffed. Make sure to press stuffing into each leg. **B**

3. Hand sew the opening at the back of the tail with a whipstitch (page 13) and orange thread, tucking in the raw edges. Start at one leg and continue to the base of the tail. Add stuffing as you sew to fill out the form completely. Repeat on the other leg. Then, begin to stitch up the sides of the tail. Add more stuffing as you go to fill it. Finally, whipstitch the bottom edge of the tail to the point, creating a round shape. **C-G**

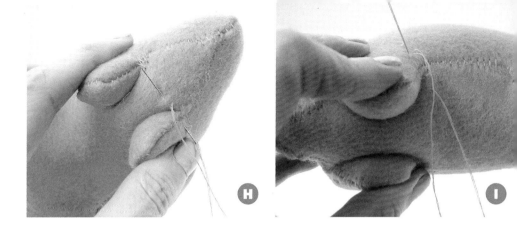

4. Add some additional stitches to improve the structure of the softie. Pinch the front legs together as shown. Add a couple of whipstitches on the creases formed, holding the legs closer to the body so the softie stands straighter. Repeat on the back legs. **H-I**

Add the Details

Add the Spines and Embroidery

1. Pair up the D pieces, right sides together. Add a dab of super glue between the pairs, then press tight to secure. Let it dry. **A-B**

Tip
I like super-gluing the spine pairs together so that there is no visible stitching around the spines. This highlights the embroidered details. If you prefer, you can sew them together with a whipstitch.

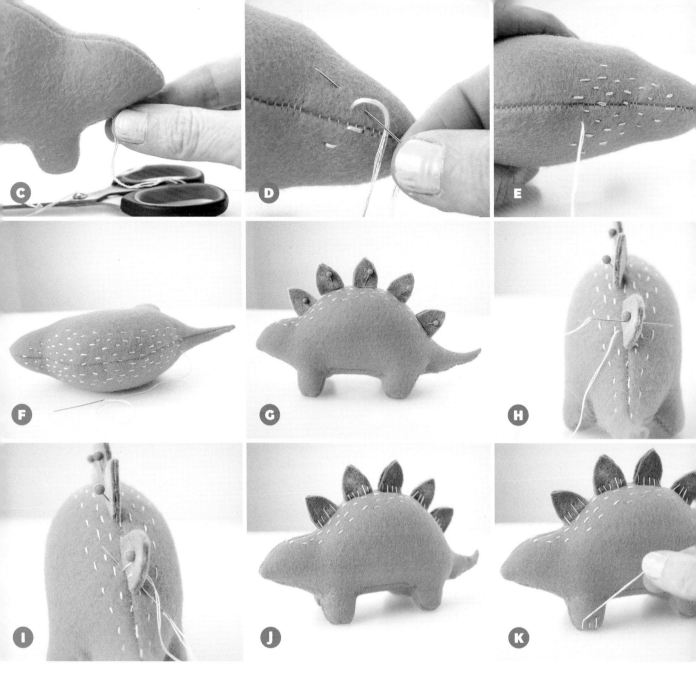

2. Thread the sewing needle with the mint green floss. Insert the needle up through the chin of the dinosaur. Seed stitch (page 21) with short vertical stitches down the whole back. **C-F**

3. Pin the spines along the center of the back as marked on the templates, or as you desire. Pin the middle spine first. **G**

4. With the mint green floss, straight stitch (page 20) each spine to the body. Alternate stitching on each side of the spine, creating 4-5 stitches on each side. **H-J**

5. Sew 3 vertical straight stitches on each foot. **K**

Add the Eyes

1. Draw the eyes with the fabric pen as marked on the pattern. **L**

2. Dip the tip of a pin into the black paint. Slowly and carefully, poke the painted end of the pin into the softie where the eye is marked. Slowly remove it. Repeat on the other eye. Let dry completely before touching to avoid smudging. **M-O**

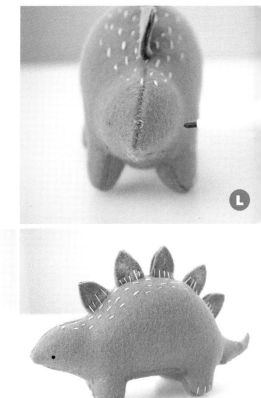

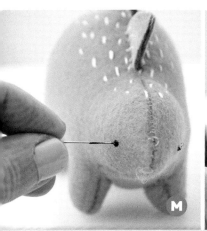

Forest Bear

This little forest bear is all about morning light, woodland walks, and rainbows. The embroidered motifs and color blocking make the possibilities for customizing this bear very exciting.

Materials

8″ × 12″ sheets of merino wool felt in mustard and rust

Scissors

Fabric pen or pencil

Sewing machine

All-purpose sewing thread in gold

Hand-sewing needle

Embroidery floss in baby pink, baby blue, navy, rust, and ivory

Sewing pins

Polyfill stuffing

Dowel rod (or similar tool)

Acrylic gouache in black

Bear templates (page 143)

TEMPLATES

Before beginning your project, print or trace the needed templates onto paper or cardstock. For this project, you need Bear Templates A–E.

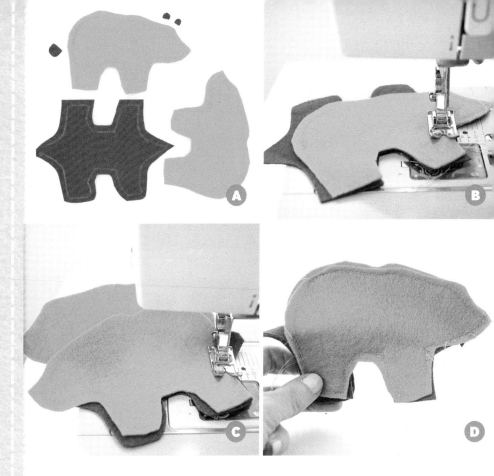

Cut & Sew

1. Trace the templates onto the felt sheet with the fabric pen. Trace pieces A and B on the mustard felt. Trace pieces C, E, and D on the rust felt. Trace 2 of piece E. Be sure to transfer over all pattern marks. Cut out the felt pieces. **A**

2. Layer piece A over piece C, right sides together and matching dots and *X*s. The tip of piece C should line up with the neck and chest of piece A. Pin if needed. Starting at the tip of piece C on the chest, sew all the way to the mark at the top of the back leg. **B**

3. Flip over the unit from Step 2. Fold piece C in half toward the bottom of the bear, then layer piece B on top (right sides together), lining up the legs and chest. Sew piece B and piece C together, starting at the mark at the top of the back leg and sewing to the end of piece C. **C**

4. Sew pieces A and B together. Start at the triangle on the butt and stitch until you slightly overlap the stitching from Steps 2 and 3. **D**

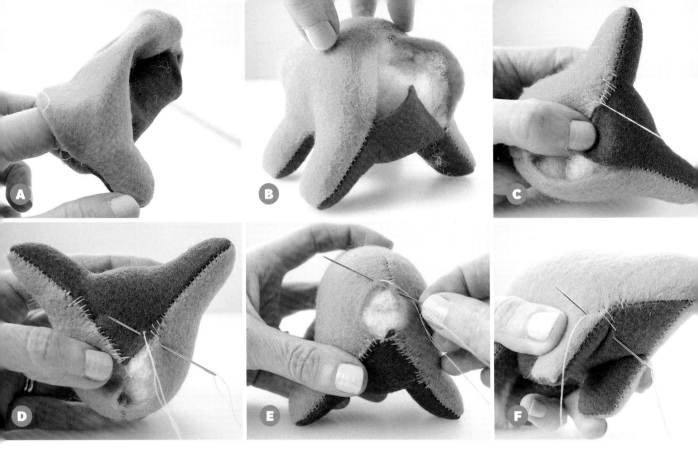

Stuff the Softie

1. Turn the bear right side out, poking out all the edges, corners, and points with the dowel rod. **A**

2. Stuff the body with polyfill. Pack it firmly, starting at the tip of the nose and working your way toward the opening until the form is well stuffed. Make sure to press stuffing into each leg. **B**

3. Hand sew the opening at the back of the bear with a whipstitch (page 13), tucking in the raw edges. Start from the bottom of the opening and work upward, sewing each leg separately. Add stuffing as you sew to fill out the form completely. You want the bear to be round and plush. Once the legs are closed stitched together, finally, whipstitch the remaining gap closed. **C-E**

4. Add some additional stitches to improve the structure of the softie. Pinch the front legs together as shown. Add a couple of whipstitches on the creases formed, holding the legs closer to the body so the softie stands straighter. Repeat on the back legs. **F**

Add the Details

Attach the Ears and Tail

1. Pin both E pieces, the ears, in place. Pin them as marked on the pattern, or adjust them as you prefer. Pin the D piece, the tail, in place on the back seam. Sew all 3 pieces to the softie with a whipstitch. **A-B**

Add the Embroidery

1. Draw the pine tree and mini rainbow design with the fabric pen around the bear's neck as shown. **C-D**

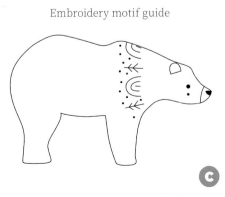

Embroidery motif guide

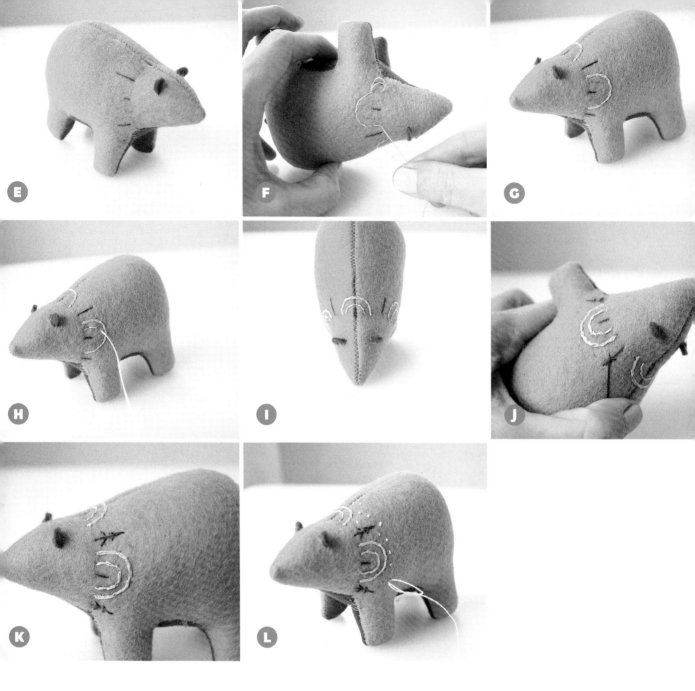

2. Stitch the pine tree trunks and the small straight stitch within each rainbow with the rust floss (see Embroidery Motif Library, page 22). Chain stitch (page 21) the outer rings of the rainbows with the baby pink floss. Chain stitch the inner rings of the rainbows with the baby blue floss. Straight stitch the pine tree leaves with the navy floss. **E–K**

3. Seed stitch (page 21) a few dots around the embroidered collar with the ivory floss. **L**

Add the Face

1. With the baby blue floss, insert the needle through the snout seam from top to bottom. Loop the thread around half of the snout, then again inserting it through the seam from top to bottom. Repeat on the other side of the snout. **M-N**

2. With the navy floss, stitch a few overlapping horizontal straight stitches to make a triangle nose. **O-P**

3. Draw the eyes with the fabric pen as marked on the pattern. **Q**

4. Dip the tip of a pin into the black paint. Slowly and carefully, poke the painted end of the pin into the softie where the eye is marked. Slowly remove it. Repeat on the other eye. Let dry completely before touching to avoid smudging. **R**

5. With the pink floss, add tiny straight stitches on either side of the face to create the impression of blush. Insert the needle on one side of the face, and bring it out on the other. Repeat moving in the opposite direction, inserting it and bringing it out right next to the original stitch. **S-T**

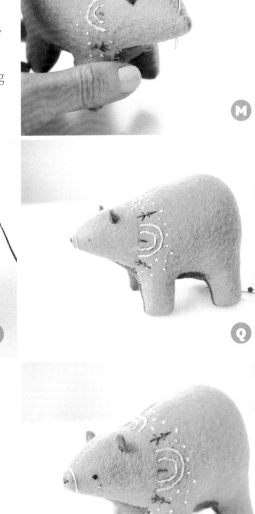

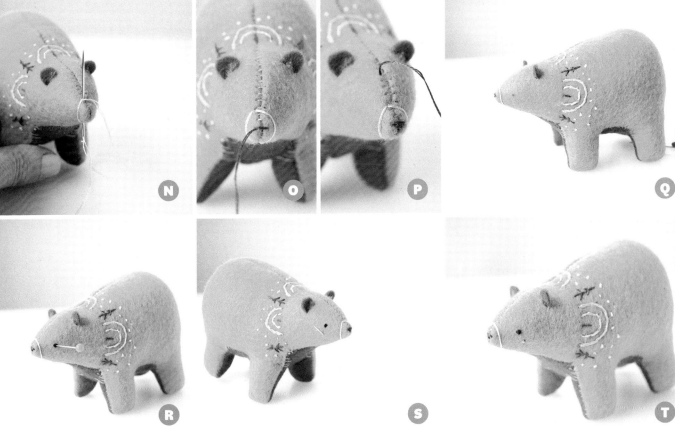

Templates

If you prefer, you can access the templates as a downloadable PDF by scanning the QR code or going to
tinyurl.com/11608-patterns-download

Embroidery Motif Templates

Sweeping Coral Branch

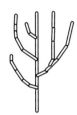

Fringed Coral Branch

Anemone Coral

Star Coral

Spiral Coral

Pine Tree

Mini Rainbow

Thistle

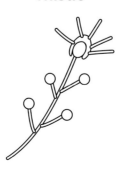

Berries

Aster

Mushroom

Dandelion

Branch

Softie Templates

Cut on solid black lines only.

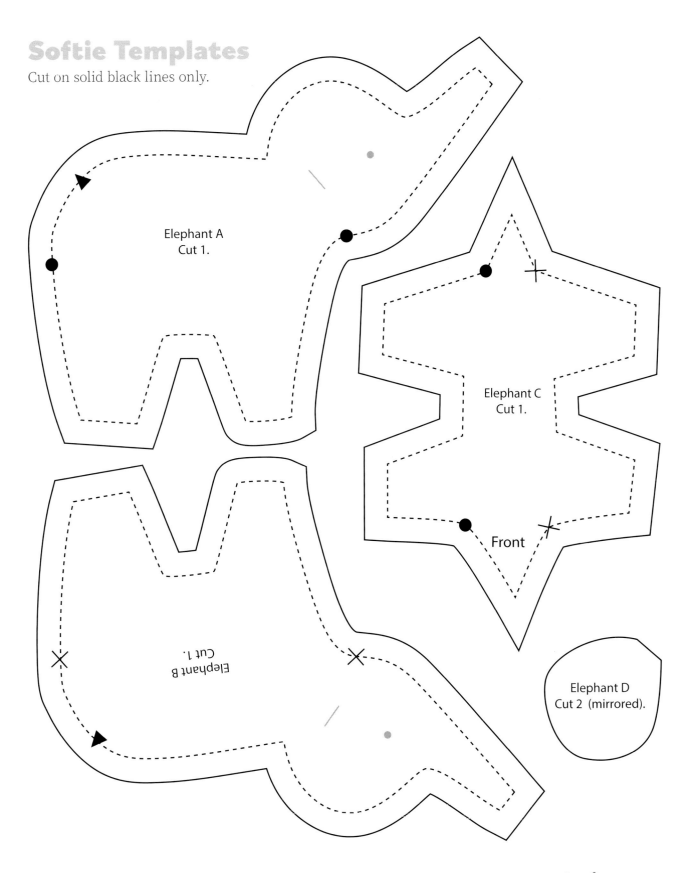

Elephant A
Cut 1.

Elephant C
Cut 1.

Front

Elephant B
Cut 1.

Elephant D
Cut 2 (mirrored).

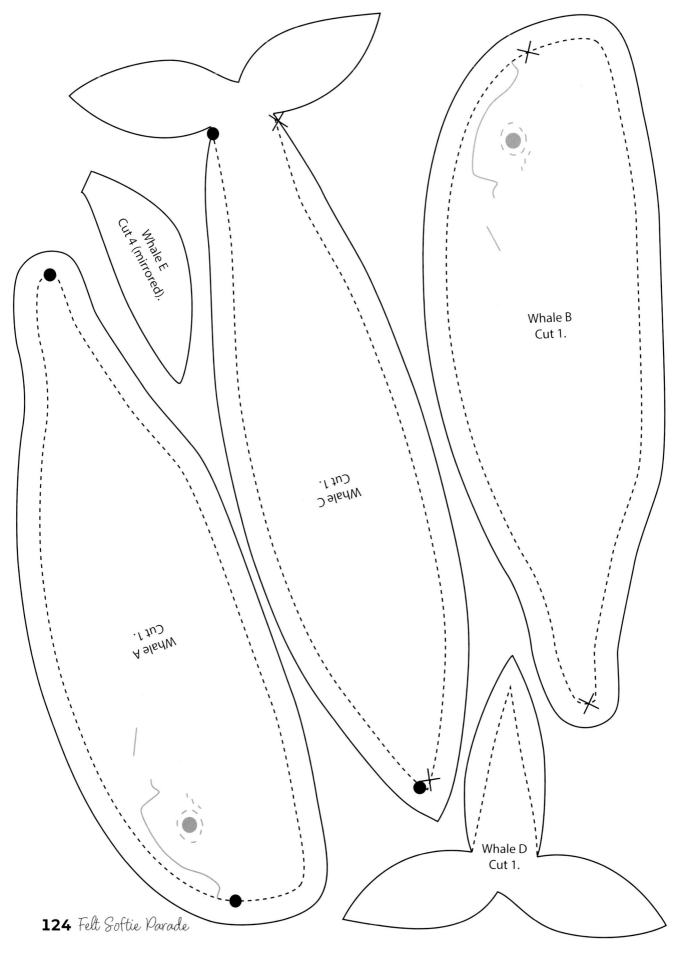

Whale E
Cut 4 (mirrored).

Whale B
Cut 1.

Whale C
Cut 1.

Whale A
Cut 1.

Whale D
Cut 1.

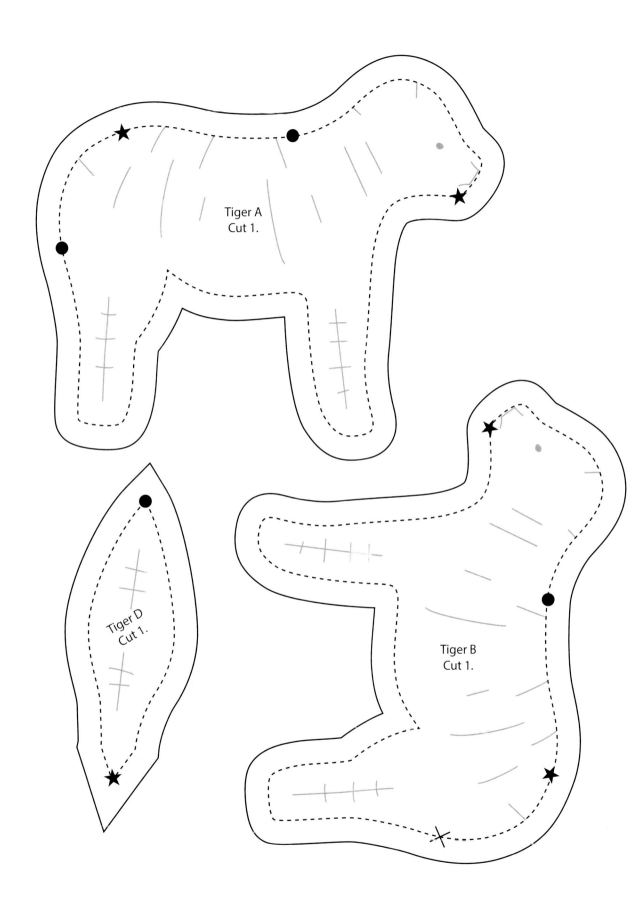

Tiger A
Cut 1.

Tiger D
Cut 1.

Tiger B
Cut 1.

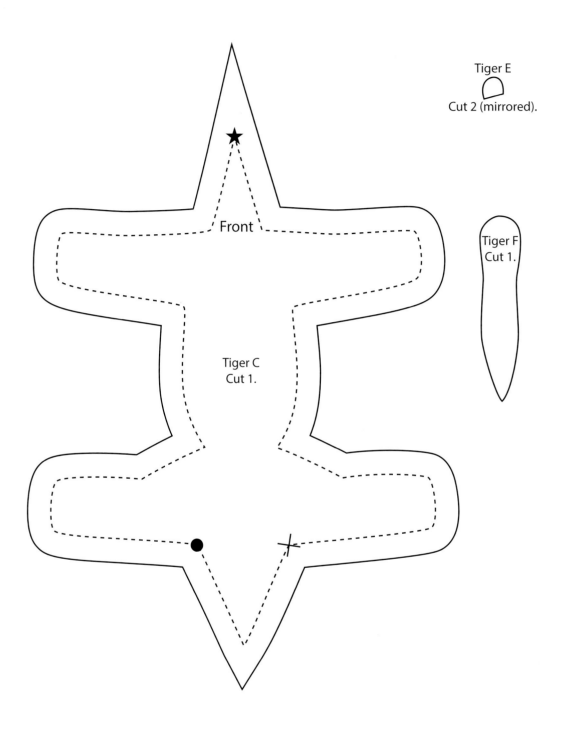

Tiger E
Cut 2 (mirrored).

Tiger F
Cut 1.

Front

Tiger C
Cut 1.

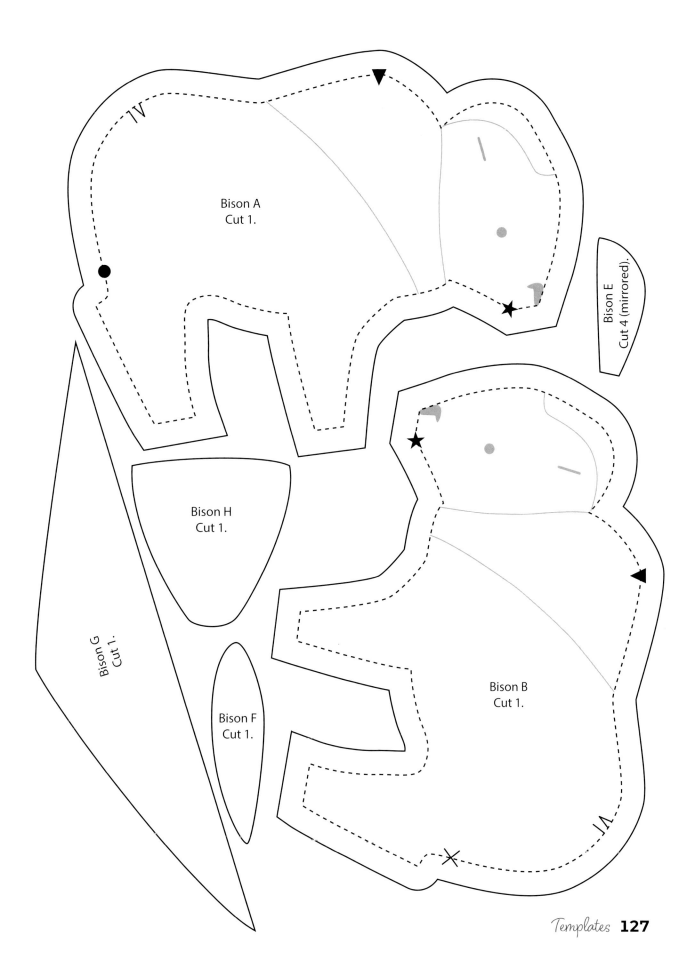

Bison A
Cut 1.

Bison E
Cut 4 (mirrored).

Bison H
Cut 1.

Bison G
Cut 1.

Bison F
Cut 1.

Bison B
Cut 1.

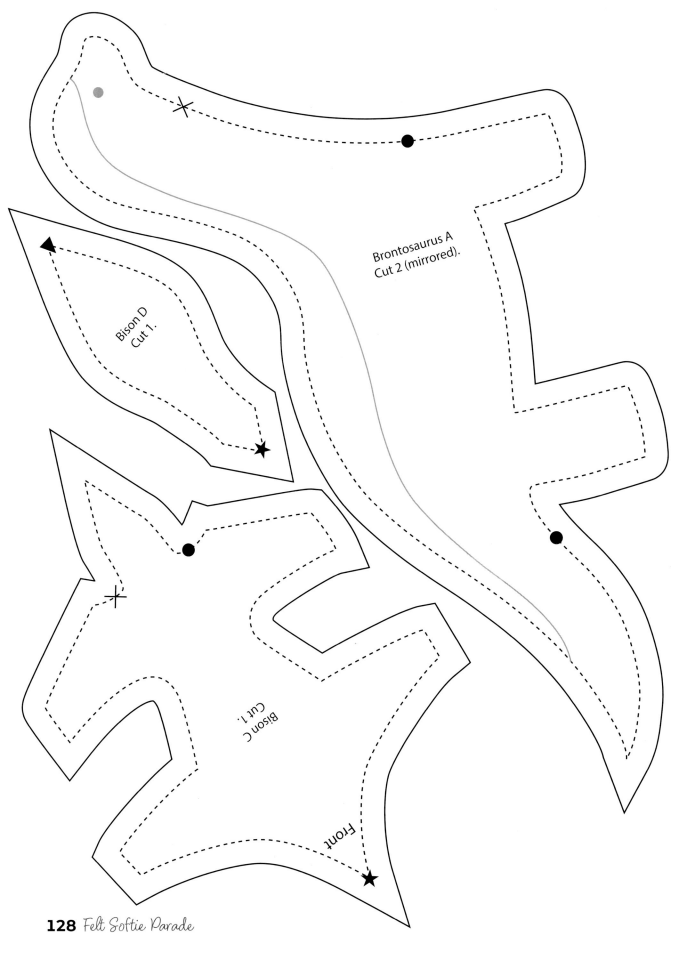

Brontosaurus A
Cut 2 (mirrored).

Bison D
Cut 1.

Bison C
Cut 1.

Front

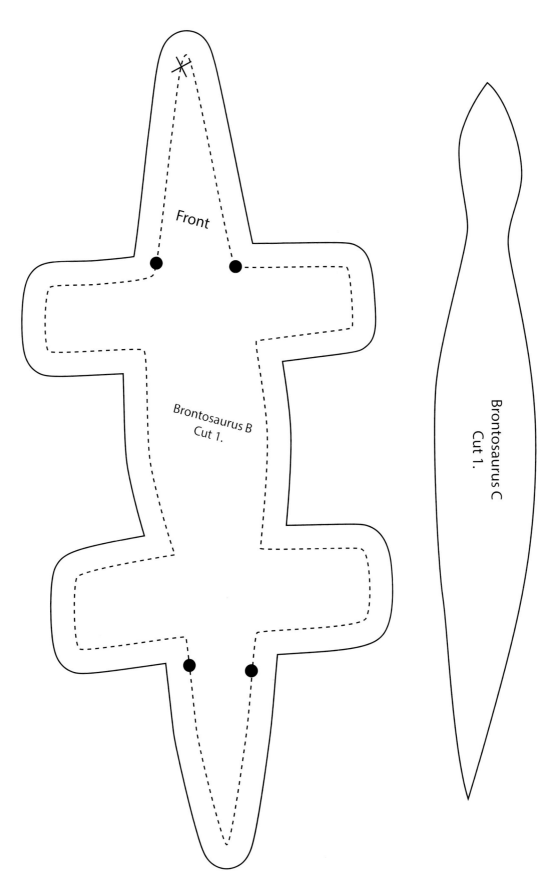

Front

Brontosaurus B
Cut 1.

Brontosaurus C
Cut 1.

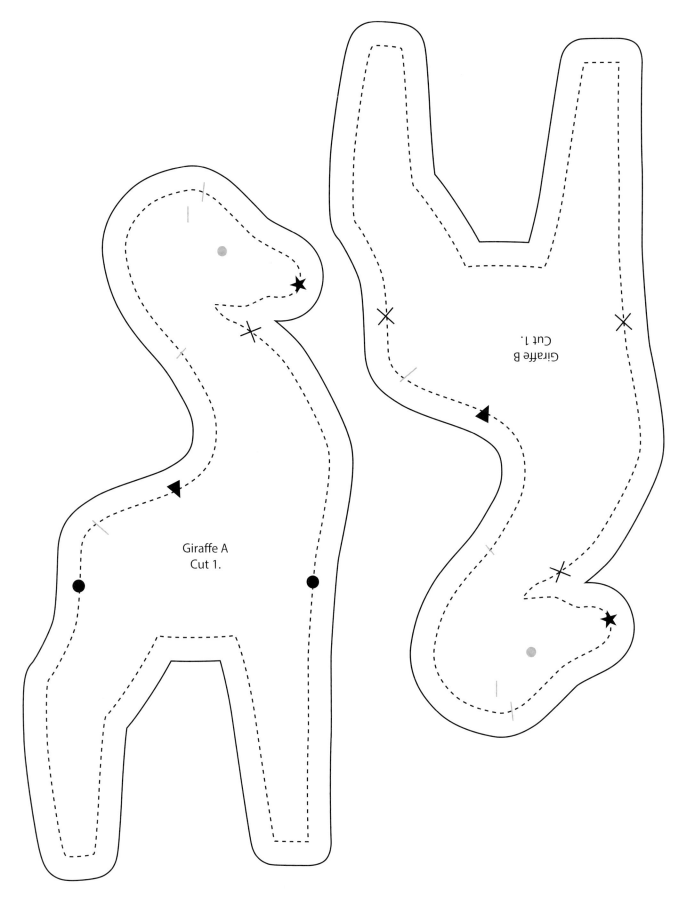

Giraffe A
Cut 1.

Giraffe B
Cut 1.

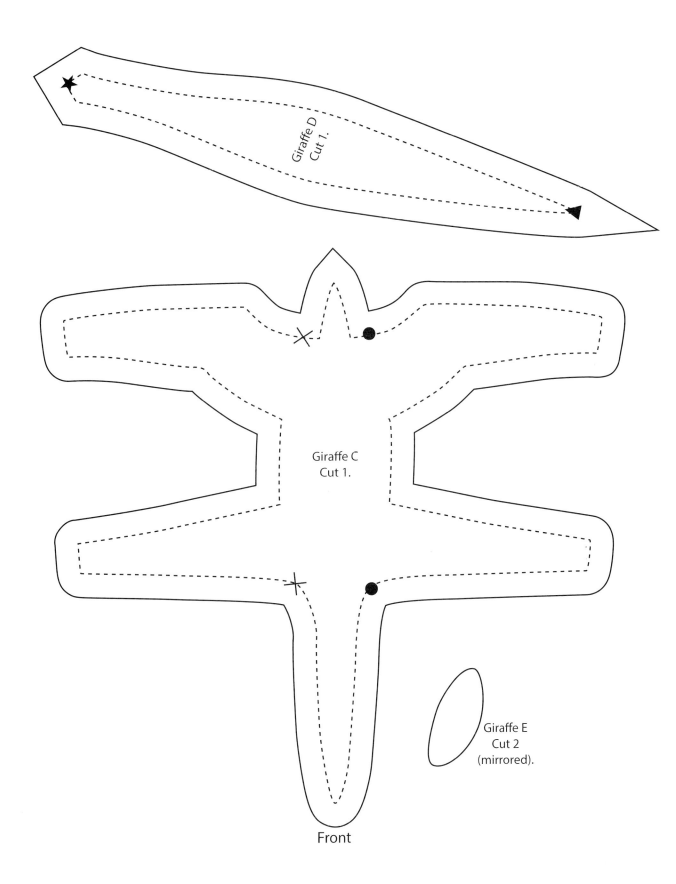

Giraffe D
Cut 1.

Giraffe C
Cut 1.

Giraffe E
Cut 2
(mirrored).

Front

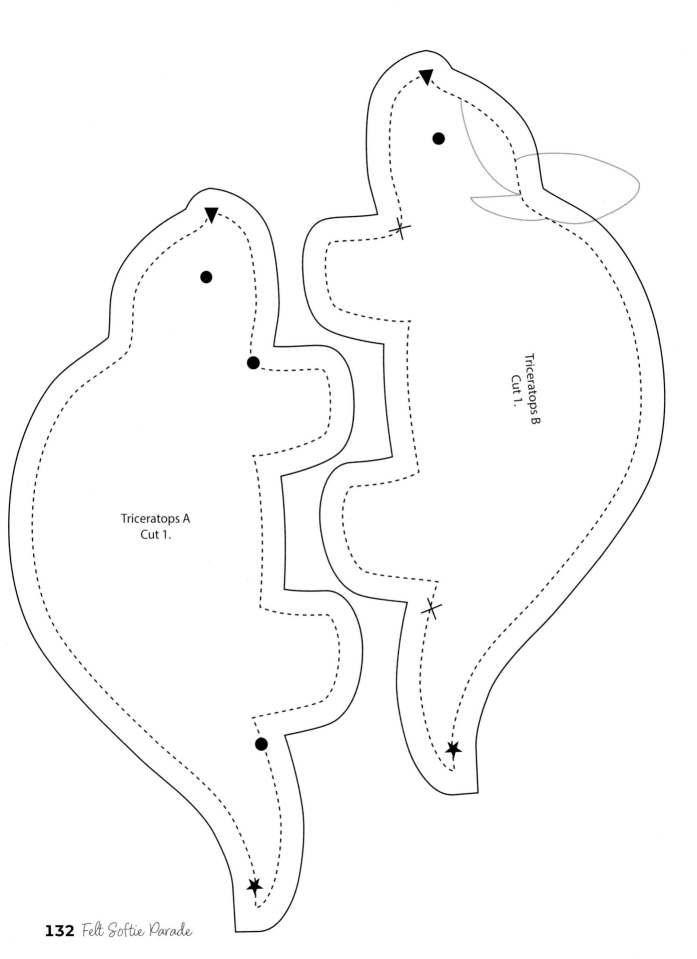

Triceratops A
Cut 1.

Triceratops B
Cut 1.

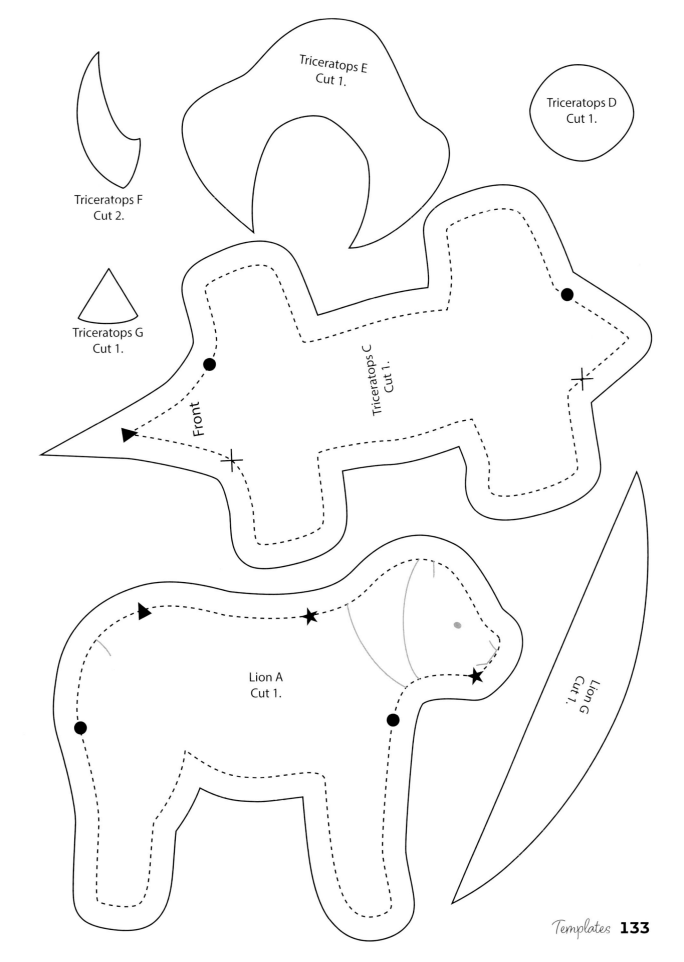

Triceratops E
Cut 1.

Triceratops D
Cut 1.

Triceratops F
Cut 2.

Triceratops G
Cut 1.

Triceratops C
Cut 1.

Front

Lion A
Cut 1.

Lion G
Cut 1.

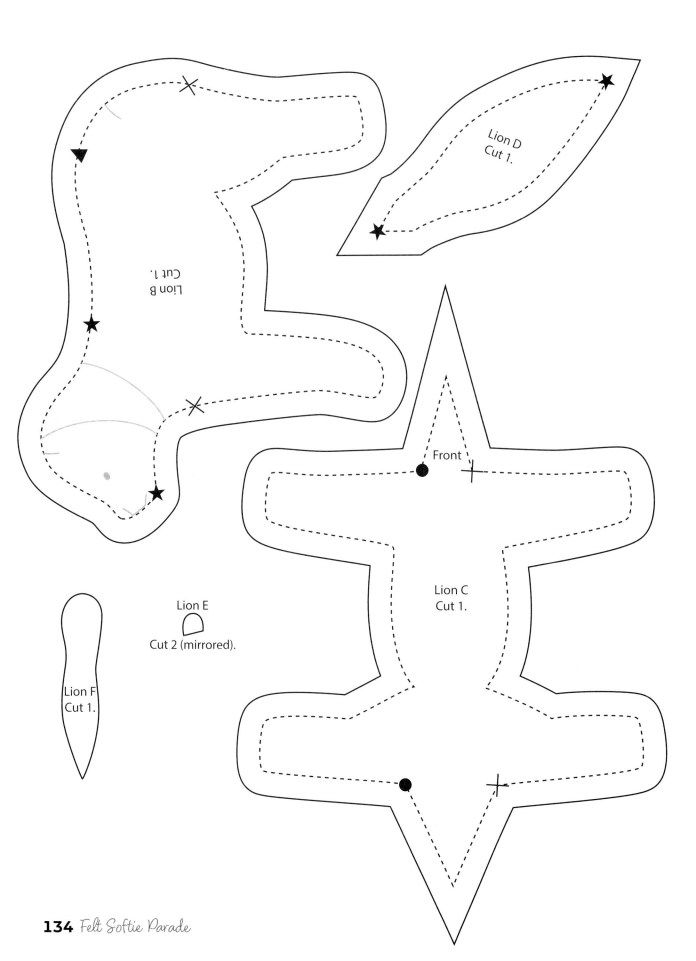

Lion D
Cut 1.

Lion B
Cut 1.

Front

Lion C
Cut 1.

Lion E
Cut 2 (mirrored).

Lion F
Cut 1.

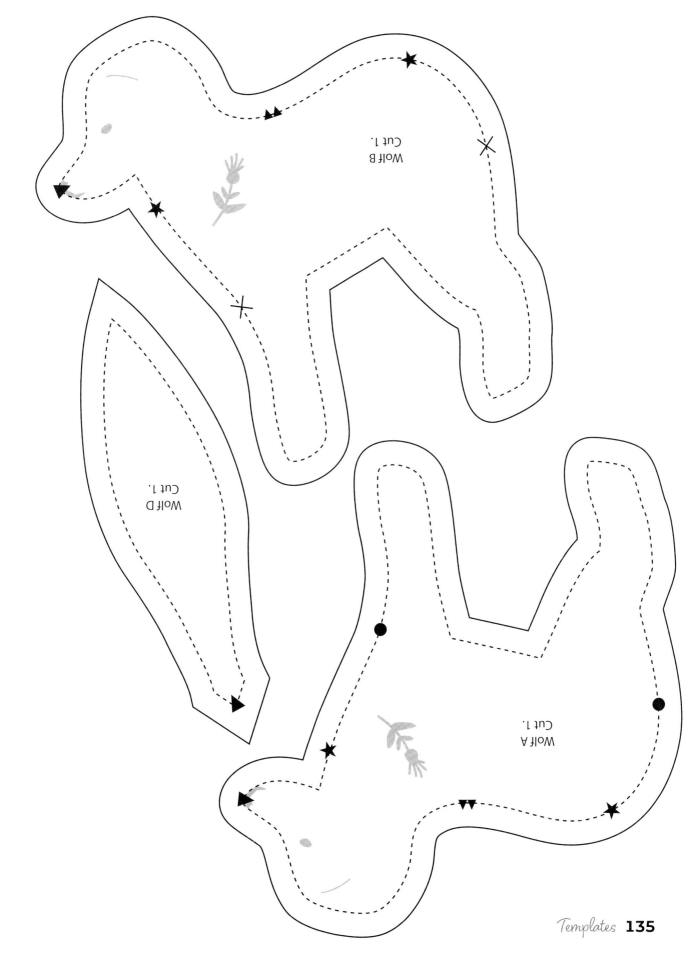

Wolf B
Cut 1.

Wolf D
Cut 1.

Wolf A
Cut 1.

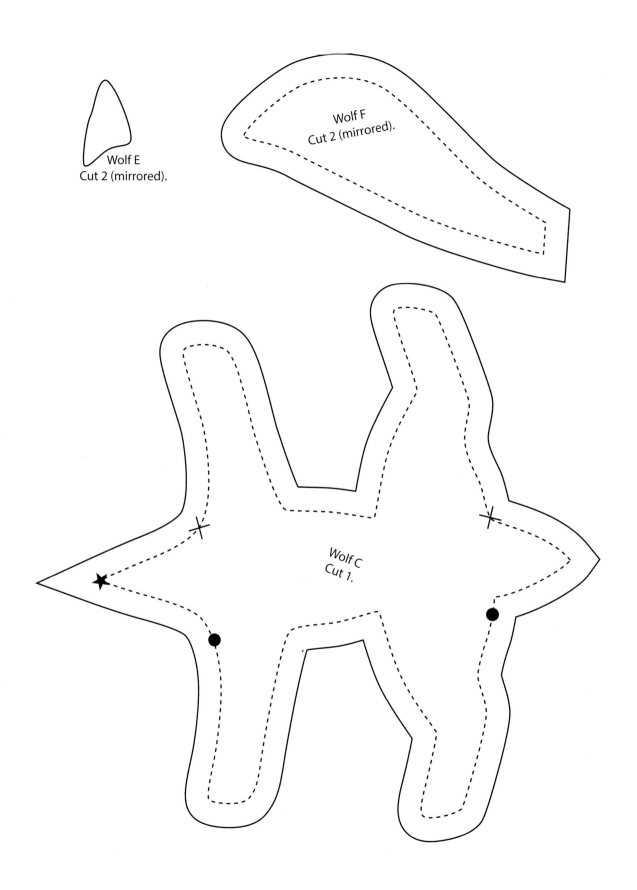

Wolf E
Cut 2 (mirrored).

Wolf F
Cut 2 (mirrored).

Wolf C
Cut 1.

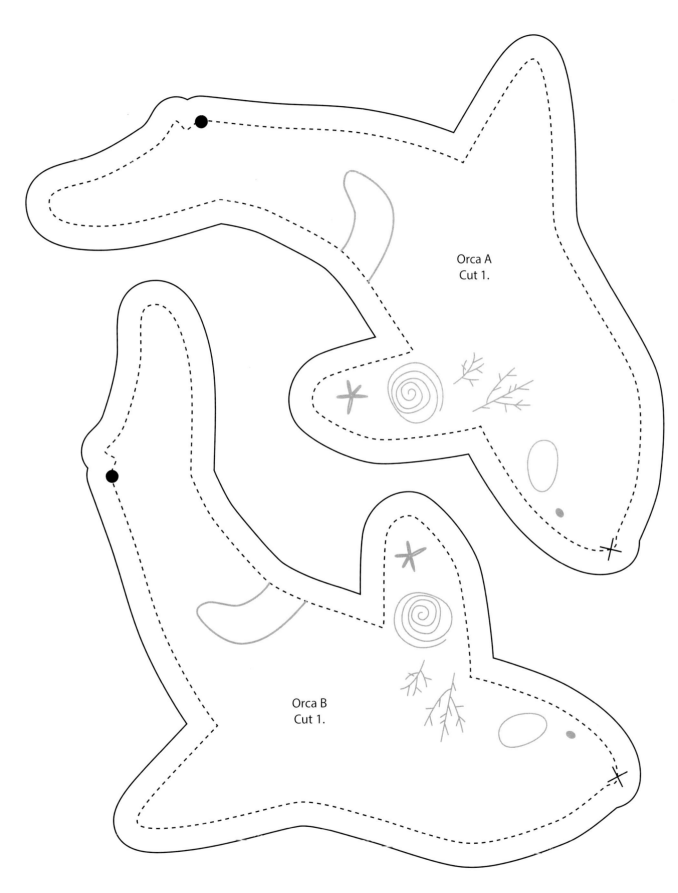

Orca A
Cut 1.

Orca B
Cut 1.

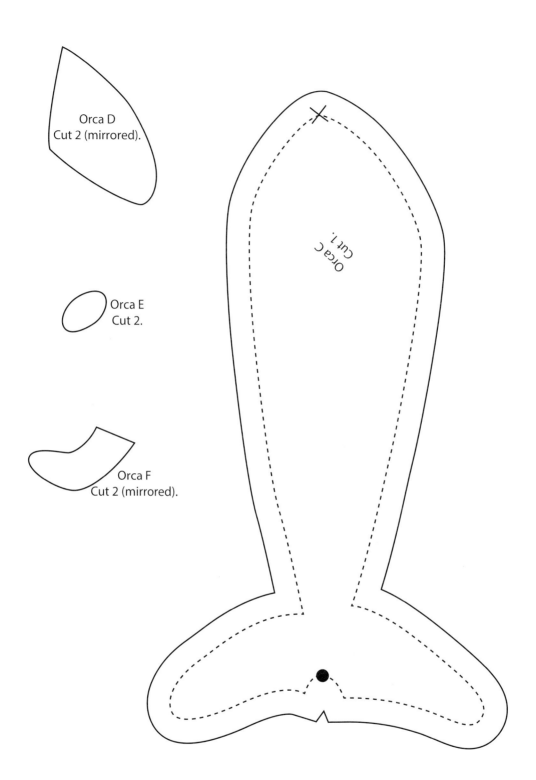

Orca D
Cut 2 (mirrored).

Orca E
Cut 2.

Orca C
Cut 1.

Orca F
Cut 2 (mirrored).

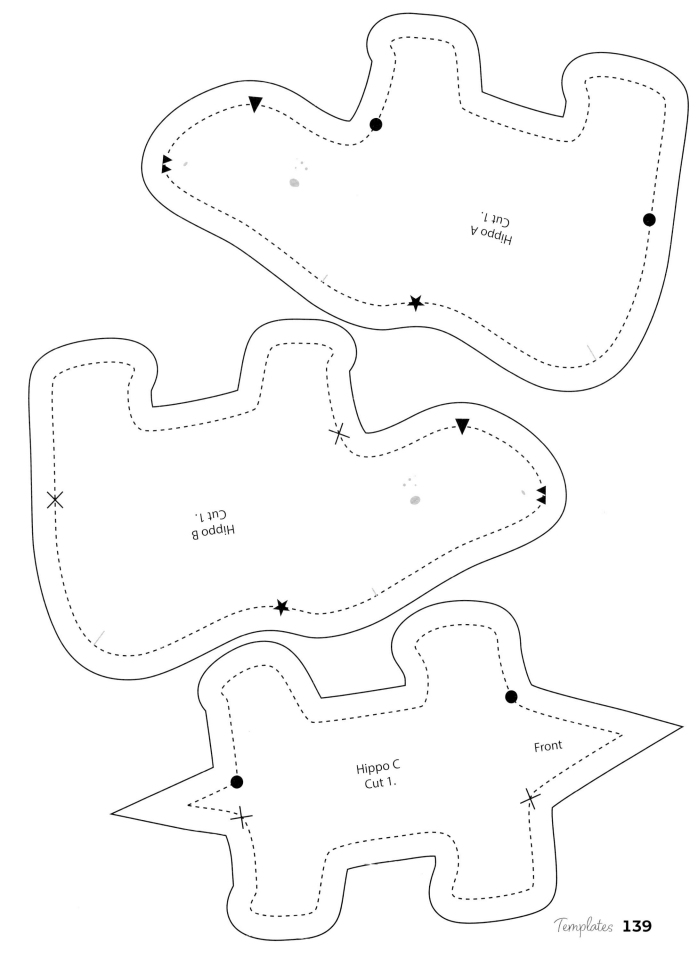

Hippo A
Cut 1.

Hippo B
Cut 1.

Hippo C
Cut 1.

Front

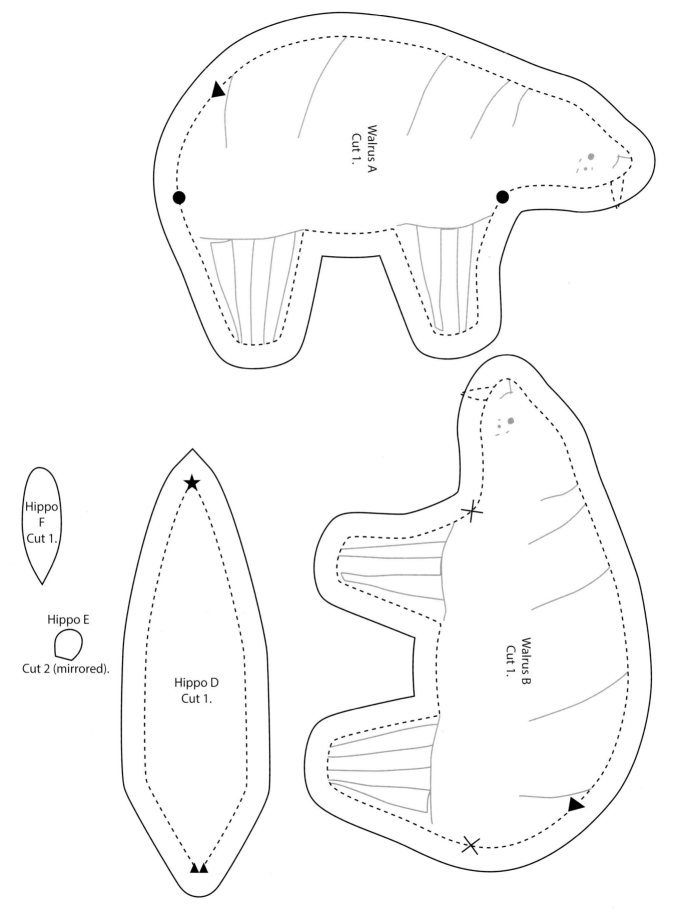

Walrus A
Cut 1.

Walrus B
Cut 1.

Hippo
F
Cut 1.

Hippo E
Cut 2 (mirrored).

Hippo D
Cut 1.

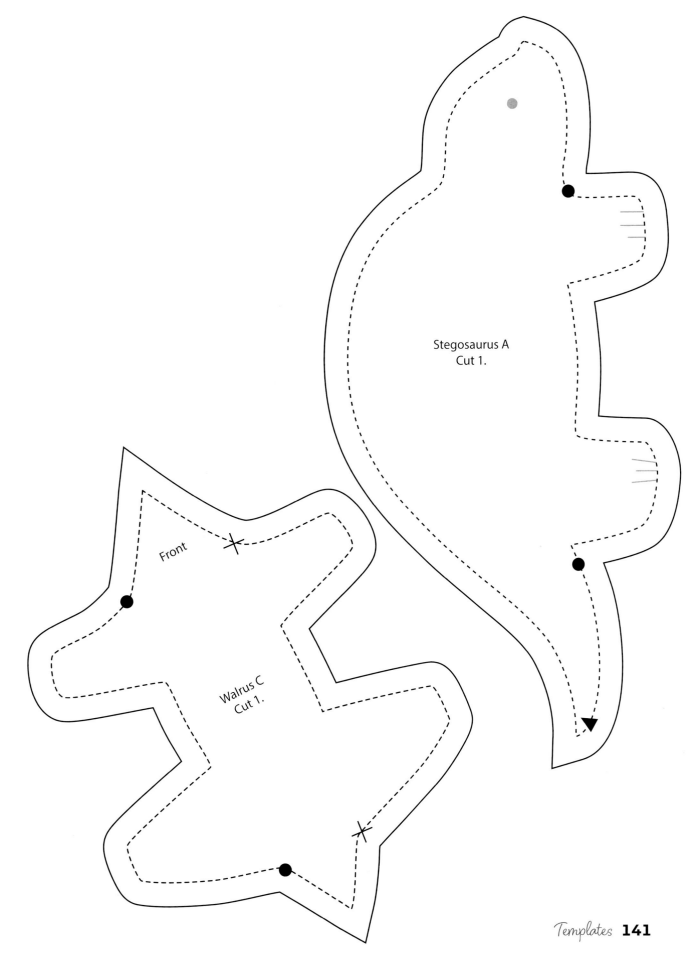

Stegosaurus A
Cut 1.

Front

Walrus C
Cut 1.

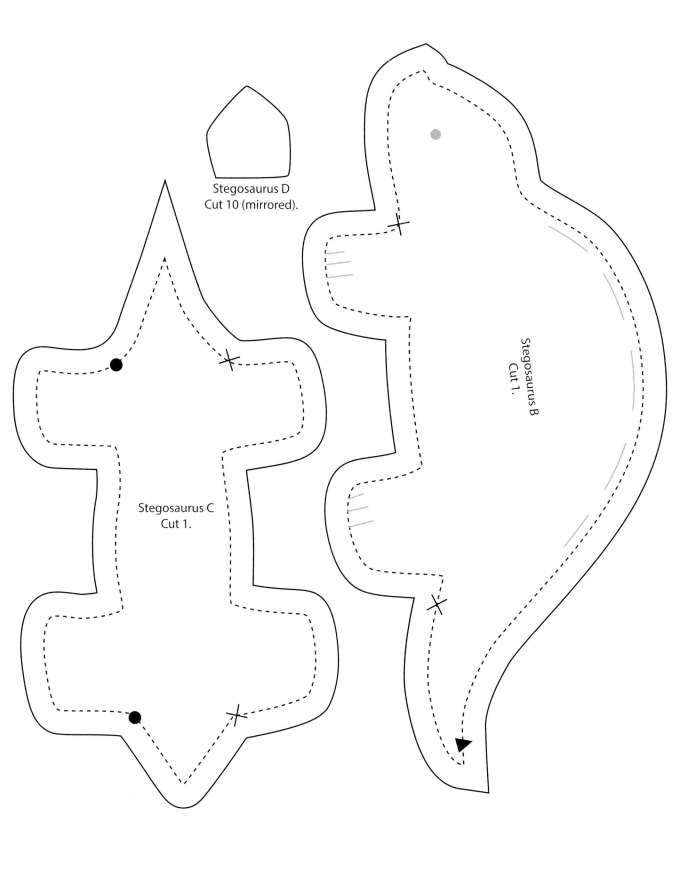

Stegosaurus D
Cut 10 (mirrored).

Stegosaurus C
Cut 1.

Stegosaurus B
Cut 1.

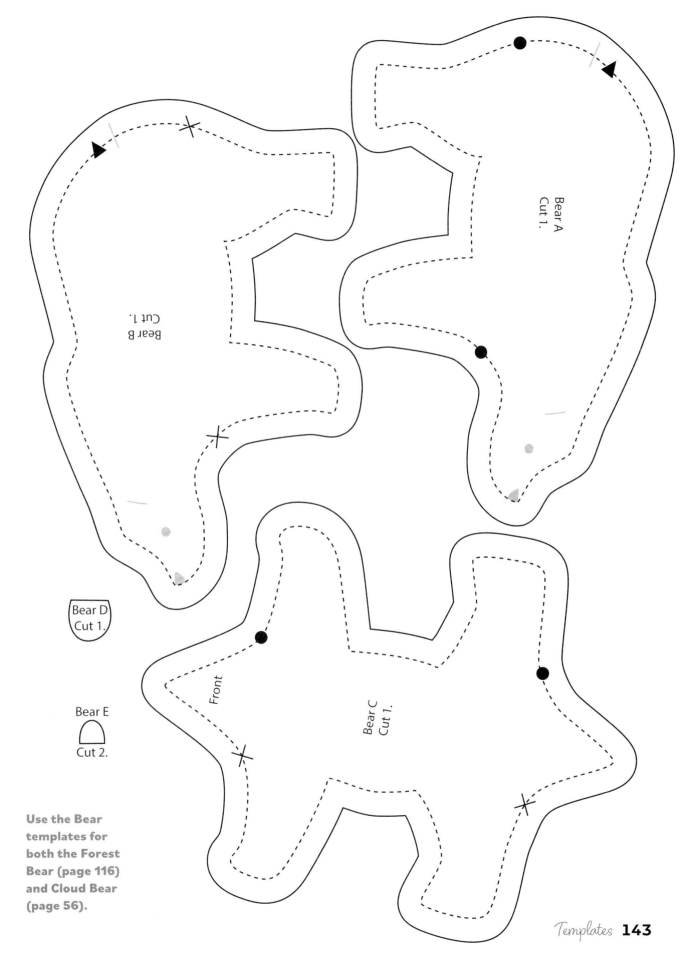

Bear A
Cut 1.

Bear B
Cut 1.

Bear D
Cut 1.

Bear E
Cut 2.

Front

Bear C
Cut 1.

Use the Bear templates for both the Forest Bear (page 116) and Cloud Bear (page 56).

About the Author

Sabina Gibson is a textile artist known for her soft sculpture animals. Telling stories through clever photography, she brings her animal characters to life in sweet handmade settings reminiscent of traditional stop motion animations from her childhood. This has earned her a large following on social media, which in turn led to many retail opportunities. In addition to her original art, she illustrates children's books and has licensed and designed many products for companies like Crate & Barrel Kids, Anthropologie, and Mattel. She is currently represented at the Catbird Literary Agency in NYC with nine children's book titles to date.

Sabina spends majority of her time creating, and when she's not in the studio she can be found in her flower gardens, making bouquets for her roadside stand. She currently resides in the Quebec countryside with her two young boys and artist husband. To see more of her work visit her website at **mountroyalmint.com** and keep up to date with all of her creative endeavors on Instagram **@mountroyalmint**